AT&T

BEYOND PHOTOGRAPHY

— THE DIGITAL DARKROOM —

Gerard J. Holzmann

AT&T Bell Laboratories
Murray Hill, New Jersey 07974

PRENTICE HALL
Englewood Cliffs, New Jersey 07632

Library of Congress Catalog Card Number: 88-5992

Prentice Hall Software Series
Brian W. Kernighan, Advisor

This book was typeset in Helvetica by the author, using an Autologic APS-5 phototypesetter and a DEC VAX 8550 running the 9th Edition of the UNIX® operating system.

Printed in the United States of America

10 9 8 7 6 5 4 3 2 1

ISBN 0-13-074410-7

Prentice-Hall International (UK) Limited, *London*
Prentice-Hall of Australia Pty. Limited, *Sydney*
Prentice-Hall Canada Inc., *Toronto*
Prentice-Hall Hispanoamericana, S.A., *Mexico*
Prentice-Hall of India Private Limited, *New Delhi*
Prentice-Hall of Japan, Inc., *Tokyo*
Simon & Schuster Asia Pte. Ltd., *Singapore*
Editora Prentice-Hall do Brasil, Ltda., *Rio de Janeiro*

Contents

First This

In more than one way this may be a confusing book. It is not about photographs and it is not about computers, at least not in the traditional way. The book shows what happens when a programmer with the ambition of a photographer and the facilities of a large research lab gets his hands on a photo digitizer and starts writing programs to transform images in every conceivable and inconceivable way. Leafing through the collection of pictures reproduced here you will probably wonder who on earth would care to go to so much trouble to create these nonsensical images. Yet these computer manipulated photographs can be fascinating. If they were not so easy to create, they might almost pass for intricate works of art. Most of the images reproduced here, however, were made in just a few seconds of computer time and startled their maker as much as the occasional viewer.

This material is just too wonderful to pass up. This book was made to share the images and the picture editing technique with more people. There's no deep message behind them, no claim on originality, and no artistic pretense. I do want to show that computer-manipulated photos do not have to be fuzzy and ugly. With some effort, and with the right tools, photos can be digitized, processed, and reproduced close to the resolution of commonly used films and photographic papers and certainly with enough detail to fool the human observer. The pictures collected here are for you to enjoy, to stare at, to feed your imagination, and to tempt you to build your own digital darkroom and duplicate the effects.

Gerard J. Holzmann

Acknowledgments

I thank all people who so courageously agreed to have their distorted portraits included in this book. Many of them have also contributed ideas for image transformations, have helped me build tools to perform them elegantly, and have forced me to keep rewriting the text until it was readable. I am particularly grateful to Jon Bentley, Brian Kernighan, and Doug McIlroy. Their careful reading of early drafts of the text helped me considerably to improve both the structure and the appearance of the book.

It is a pleasure to acknowledge also the inspiration and crucial help of Rob Pike and Ken Thompson during the development of the software. Rob Pike contributed many ideas for image transformations (including the idea for the cover picture) and helped me develop and print many versions of the negatives for the pictures reproduced in this book. Ed Sitar helped me overcome numerous problems that stand between an idea and its realization by miraculously always finding just the right piece of equipment that I needed. Andrew Hume spent more days and weeks than he would care to remember to get sensitive image processing equipment to work with our 9th Edition UNIX systems. Mary Bittrich, Beate Oestreicher, and Judy Paone helped me track down and verify much of the information presented.

Without all these people I could not have written this book. I thank them all.

GJH

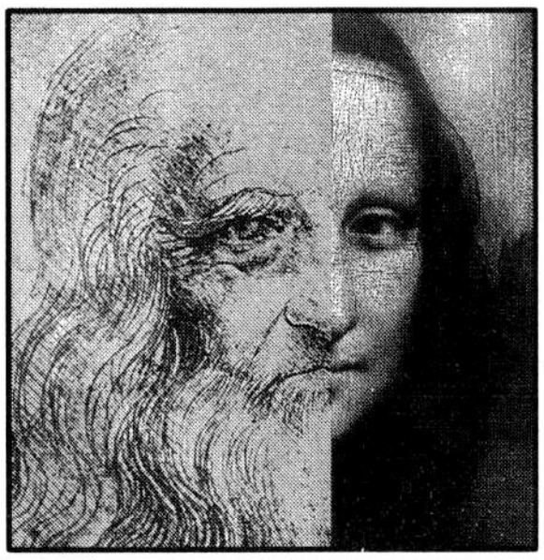

1 Beyond Photography

A couple of years ago I visited a friend who was preparing a magazine ad for publication. The ad was for the U.S. Army and it showed a small group of young people in uniform under a happy slogan. Most of the people in the group were white males. There was one woman and one black male among them. My friend's job was to retouch the photo. Apart from removing the odd pimple or freckle he was asked to raise the rank of the woman and the black male to be higher than those of their colleagues. Not only are we easy to fool, photography has made it easy for us to fool ourselves in quite subtle ways.

It didn't take long for portrait photographers to discover that even if their sparkling conversation would fail to put the twinkle in the eyes of a model, a speck of white paint could do the job. And they could really please their customers by removing bags and wrinkles, typically by scraping off the offending areas straight from the negative (called *knifing* the negative). Of course, to retouch a photo invisibly does require skill. But there's so much more that you can do with photos in a darkroom. What amateur photographer hasn't experimented with multiple exposures or solarization, if only by accident? There is in fact a rich tradition for this type of image manipulation. It is interesting to see how far back this history of tampering with photographs really goes.

How to Photograph a Ghost

Photography dates from the beginning of the nineteenth century. The oldest surviving photograph was taken by the Frenchman Joseph Nièpce in 1827. Nièpce died in 1833. His coworker Louis Daguerre continued the work, and together with Nièpce's son Isidore sold the invention to the French government on 19 August 1837. The true ancestor of today's photography, however, is not the *daguerrotype* but something called a *kalotype.* This method, the first to use photographic negatives, was patented by the Englishman William Henry Fox Talbot in 1841.

What must have been the first exhibition of photographic portraits was organized in August 1840 by a Swiss painter named Johann Isenring. The portraits were hand colored, and, says a French history book* to our satisfaction, Isenring showed the photos

> *après avoir gratté la pupille des yeux sur la plaque pour donner vie à ses personnages. — after having scratched the pupils of the eyes on the photographic plate to bring the images to life.*
>
> *Histoire de la photographie (p. 24)*

So, not much time was lost in the attempt to perfect perfection. And it was not an exception either. Dawn Ades, for instance, writes:

> *It was common practice in the nineteenth century to add figures to a landscape photograph, and to print in a different sky. The latter type of 'combination printing' was to compensate for the defects in early cameras, because it was almost impossible [...] to obtain in one exposure both sharp foreground detail and impressive meteorological effects.*
>
> *Photomontage (p. 89)*

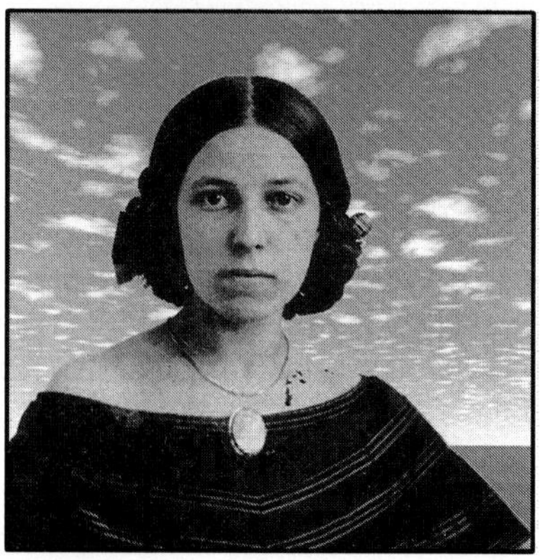

Combination Print

By 1859 the now familiar technique of double exposure had been described in detail by the English photographer Henry Peach Robinson, in a booklet with the revealing title *"On printing photographic pictures from several negatives."* Double exposure proved to be a convincing way to demonstrate the existence of ghosts in the late nineteenth century. The procedure was as follows. A photographic plate was pre-exposed with the desired image of a forefather. Then, in the presence of an objective audience, the real picture was taken (on

* Complete references can be found at the end of this chapter.

the same plate) and developed. Out came a photo of the scene that had just been photographed with the image of the ghost in the background.

Not everybody was happy with this photographic trickery. In 1856 a series of angry letters appeared in the *Journal of the London Photographic Society*, protesting the doctoring of photographs. In particular, these writers wanted retouched photographs banned from all exhibitions of the society. Aaron Scharf writes:

> *...retouching had reached such proportions, it seems, that it became difficult to find photographs which had not been embellished by hand.*
>
> *Creative Photography (p. 14)*

The protests were, of course, to no avail. Distorting or enhancing photographs remained a popular pastime, as illustrated by the following selection of books from that period:

1861 – Alfred Wall, *"A manual of artistic colouring as applied to photographs."* – A first description of the still popular method of hand coloring black-and-white photographs.

1866 – Antoine Claudet, *"A new means of creating harmony and artistic effect in photographic portraits."* – The method consisted of changing the focus of the lens during an exposure. After all, exposure times were still long enough.

1869 – Henry Peach Robinson, *"Pictorial effect in photography."* – A detailed description of combination printing methods, for instance by using special cloud negatives.

1889 – Jacques Ducos du Hauron, *"Photographie transformiste."* – A most entertaining booklet on photographic distortion techniques. It describes methods to make photographic caricatures, using cylindrical mirrors, conically shaped negatives, tilted printing paper, or by using special lenses that change the image during exposures. It even includes a discussion of a sophisticated technique for separating the emulsion from a photographic plate and reshaping it to achieve special effects.

1893 – Bergeret & Drouin, *"Les recreations photographiques."* – An encyclopedia of techniques for photographic image manipulations.

1896 – Walter Woodbury, *"Photographic amusements."* – A book that featured, for instance, a technique called *multiphotography*. The method was simply to use mirrors to photograph someone from several angles at the same time. The book was printed in no fewer than 11 editions between 1896 and 1937.

Composite portraits have also been popular for quite some time. The simple composite of the Mona Lisa and a self-portrait of Leonardo da Vinci shown on the first page of this chapter is a recent example. It was used by artist Lillian Schwartz to support a theory that the Mona Lisa could be another self-portrait of da Vinci. Ewing and McDermott wrote in the introduction to an entertaining book on photo composites by Nancy Burson:

> *Francis Galton, a biologist, founder of eugenics, and cousin of Charles Darwin, probably made the first composite photographs in 1877. Caught up in the nineteenth century's passion for the classification of types, he hoped*

to make pictures of the average criminal, the consumptive patient, the military officer, and so on.

Composites (p. 12)

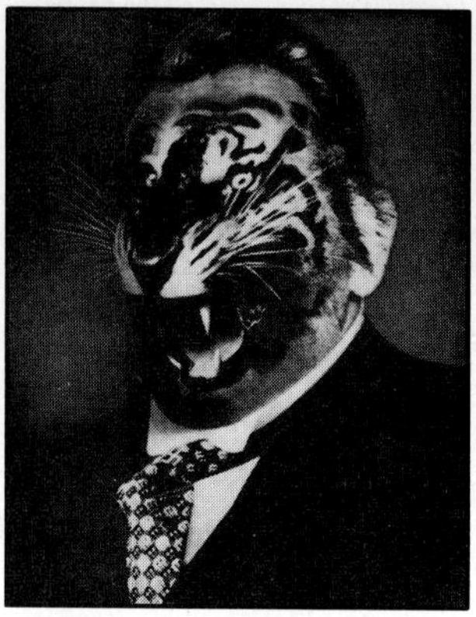

John Heartfield (1931)

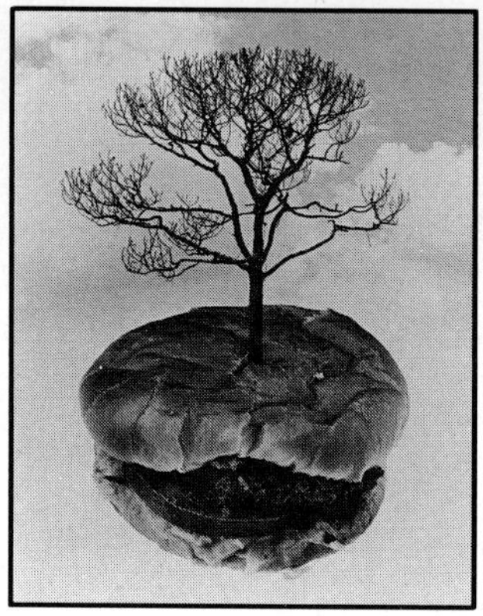

Jerry Uelsmann (1970)

Around 1920, John Heartfield and George Grosz of the Berlin *Dada* group were among the first to use photocollage and photomontage artistically. Heartfield became famous for his fierce photomontages directed against the rise of Hitler in Germany. Today, of course, image manipulation is as popular as ever, though much less debated. In Germany, artist Klaus Staeck follows in Heartfield's footsteps by using photomontage as a political weapon in his work. In America, photographer Jerry Uelsmann has perfected combination printing with modern darkroom techniques. He makes impressive works using up to six enlargers for a single print.

From Isenring in 1840 to Uelsmann today, photomontage has made quite a history. If anything, it shows that almost anything can be done and has been done to change a photographic image.

Why Bother with Computers?

If almost everything can and has been done in conventional darkrooms, why should we even bother trying to use computers? There are two main reasons. First of all, everything one can do to a digitized picture with a computer is reversible, which makes it much easier to play around with a picture, trying different transformations. Second, not only can the computer mimic everything a skilled professional can do with chemicals and enlargers in a darkroom, it can indeed also do things that are almost impossible to do any other way. How would you smoothly fade a picture from a negative to a positive version in a darkroom? In a darkroom you can correct perspective by tilting the enlarger lens or the printing paper, but how do you hold the paper to twist a picture into a spiral? Believe it or not, to a certain extent you can even restore the focus in a fuzzy picture or remove motion blur with a computer. Less than half of the image transformations shown in Chapter **4** can be done in a conventional darkroom, and only with considerably more effort.

So, there's a lot to be said for using the computer as a digital darkroom. Besides, there are a few other and perhaps even more convincing reasons for using a computer darkroom: you never get your hands wet, you *can* but do not *have* to turn off the light, and it can be very entertaining.

An Overview

In the next few chapters we will explore the new world of digital photography and the type of image manipulation it makes possible.

In Chapter 2 we will see what type of hardware you would need to equip a computer as a darkroom. You need some way to get the picture into the computer, with a digitizer or a frame-grabber. And you need some way to print it back on film or paper with a printer. Once the image is in the computer, nothing stops you from turning it inside out. Beware, you will soon find out what this means. For this you need software, and this is where it gets really interesting.

Chapter 3 explains in detail how we can build a language for defining image transformations. The picture processing language serves as an example of the new types of digital darkroom tools that the photographer of the future may use. It shows how you can filter, enhance, and transform images without having to worry much about the theory that is behind it all.

Chapter 4 presents an array of maltreated pictures that illustrate the new possibilities. Each picture is accompanied by a brief explanation of how the effect was achieved.

Chapter 5 gives complete details on how to build a digital darkroom on your own personal computer and reproduce almost everything discussed in this book.

The book concludes with a catalogue of useful transformations that is presented in Chapter 6.

Books Mentioned

Some of the books mentioned in the text are listed below. Not all books, however, are still in print.

Composites, Nancy Burson, Richard Carling, and David Kramlich, Beech Tree Books, New York, 1986, ISBN-0-688-02601-X.

Creative Photography, Aaron Scharf, Reinhold Publishing, New York, 1965, Library of Congress #65-13370.

Die Kunst findet nicht im Saale statt, Klaus Staeck, Rowohlt Verlag, Hamburg, 1976, ISBN 3-498-06114-3.

Fantastic Photographs, Attilio Colombo, Random House, New York, 1979, ISBN 0-860-92017-8.

John Heartfield Leben und Werk, Wieland Herzfelde, VEB Verlag der Kunst,

Dresden, 3rd printing 1986, LSV-8116.

Histoire de la photographie, Jean A. Keim, Presses Universitaires de France, Paris, 1970.

Photomontage, Dawn Ades, Thames and Hudson, London, 1976, ISBN 0-500-27080-5.

Silver Meditations, Jerry N. Uelsmann, Morgan & Morgan Publishing, Dobbs Ferry, N.Y., 1975, ISBN 0-871-00087-3.

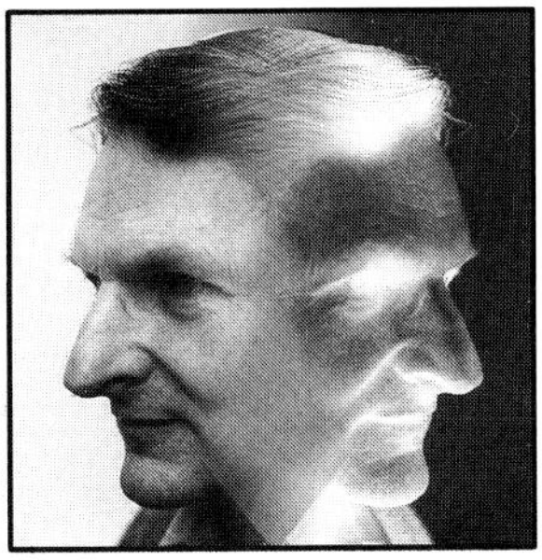

2 Image Processing

One of the first machines that was specifically built to translate a photograph into a digital code was the Bartlane cable picture transmission system from the early 1920s. In about three hours the Bartlane system could transmit a photo from New York to London, with sufficient resolution to allow the photo to be printed in a newspaper. Image processing with computers did not start until the sixties, when the first lunar probes were launched. Somehow the people at NASA's Jet Propulsion Lab in Pasadena were able to transform the fuzzy and distorted little pictures returned by the Ranger and Surveyer spacecraft into the detailed images that hit the pages of *Life* magazine. How was this done? There is in fact quite some theory behind these image enhancements. The good news, however, is that the process is by now so standardized that it can be translated into a small set of "digital darkroom tools" that can be used and understood by anyone.

Digital Photos

Computers work well with numbers, and they can in principle handle any problem that can be translated into numbers. This is not just true for problems with a mathematical flavor. It is also true for photos. A photograph, after all, is just a large collection of dots on a piece of paper. Each dot can have a brightness and perhaps a color. The number of possible dots, brightness values, and colors can be large, but is usually limited. This means that any photo can be translated into numbers and stored in a computer. How many numbers does it take to define a photo? In the next chapter we will see that roughly 20 million numbers can record *all* the information on a single 35mm black-and-white negative, where each number has a value between 0 and 255. Since this is quite a fixed number, we can even calculate the maximum number of different pictures that can be made on a 35mm negative. It is estimated that all photographers, amateur and professional together, take about 10 billion or 10^{10} pictures per year. The maximum possible number of pictures is $256^{20,000,000}$. At our current rate, then, we will not run out of things to photograph for another $10^{48,164,799}$ years, give or take a few.

It is actually remarkable that we can translate (digitize) a photograph, any photograph, into a set of numbers without losing information. The numbers are much like a negative: at any time they can be used to recreate the original image. But better still, these digital negatives are much easier to store. They do not age or fade, and they can be manipulated just as easily in a computer as real negatives can be manipulated in a darkroom. It is not unlikely that within the next ten years the conventional camera we all use today will be replaced by a *digital* camera that takes photos on a floppy disk that is "processed" in a normal personal computer with the type of software presented in this book. The photos can be shown on a television set or printed with a high-resolution film printer that may someday be as standard as the dot matrix printer of a personal computer today.

There are signs that this development is under way. Equipment for image recording and replay has over the years become smaller and smaller, so much so that the difference in size between the latest video "camcorders" and a normal SLR (single-lens reflex) photo camera has become almost negligible. In the fall of 1986 companies such as RCA, Hitachi, NEC, and Toshiba introduced the first digital video recorders that internally sample and digitize video images. So far, the digital capabilities of these recorders are used mostly for special effects such as high-quality freeze frame, slow motion, and "insert pictures" (a second video image inserted in the corner of the screen). The move, however, is in the direction of a completely digital video system, and with that it will become very easy to hook up a video recorder to a computer and capture video images on a computer disk.

Digital Cameras

Digital SLR cameras have been in development for almost ten years. It first became possible to build these cameras with the availability of large CCD arrays. The CCD or charge-coupled device was invented by Willard S. Boyle and George E. Smith at Bell Labs in the early 1970s (the patent is dated December 31, 1974). It works much like a photocell, translating brightness values into electrical signals. By packing thousands of these CCD elements onto a chip, a solid-state image sensor can be constructed that can almost instantly sample an image and encode it into an electrical or even a digital signal. The first application of the CCD image sensors was in solid-state video and television cameras. The resolution of the image sensor depends trivially on the number of CCD elements in the array. The largest CCD device currently available is a 2048×2048 array made by Tektronix, Inc. It measures 2.5 inches square, which makes it also the largest integrated circuit made to date.

The CCD image sensors have a number of important advantages over other types of photo detectors, and even over conventional photographic film. First, they have a much higher quantum efficiency, that is, they are more sensitive to light. They also have a superior linearity and a large dynamic range, which means that there is a simple fixed relation between the brightness of an image and the response of a CCD element for a wide range of brightness values. Finally, the CCD sensors produce a high-quality and stable signal, with very little noise. They have, in fact, only one real disadvantage. The larger cells are still hard to make and are therefore expensive.

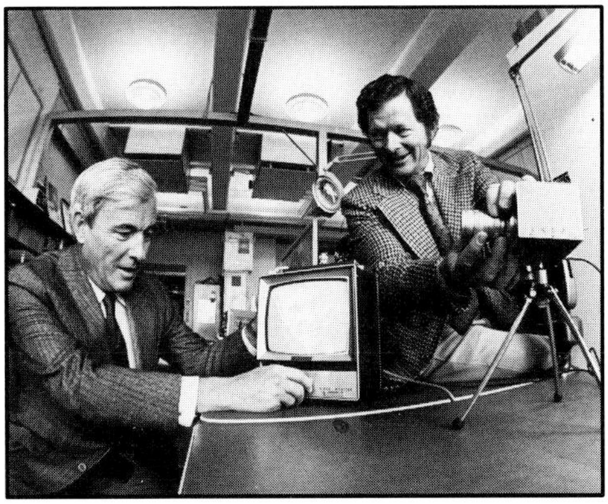

Willard S. Boyle (l.) and George E. Smith
Demonstration of the First CCD Camera in Dec. 1974

The first truly digital cameras for making photographs have yet to be built. Kodak's subsidiary Videk has developed a high-resolution black-and-white CCD camera, named the *Megaplus*, that comes close to a such a general purpose digital camera. The camera is built around a 1340×1037 dot image sensor and produces digital output. So far, though, the Megaplus camera has no independent image storage capability; it is meant to be used as a scanner with a fixed connection to a personal computer. The first version being marketed by Videk is also quite expensive (over $10,000). It has, however, all the features of a serious forerunner of the digital camera of the future.

A low-resolution alternative to a fully digital camera is already available today: the still video camera. It has a CCD image sensor, it records photos on floppy disk instead of film, and in fact the only difference from a real digital camera is that it is based on video technology rather than computer technology. Let us look in a little more detail at some of these cameras, though it is good to keep in mind that they cannot compete with the price and resolution of conventional photo cameras and films just yet.

Still Video Cameras

Several large companies, most notably Canon, Fuji, Kodak, and Sony, have developed, or are in the process of developing, a new generation of SLR photo cameras using CCD image sensors and video technology. In 1980 Sony demonstrated the first "still video image" camera, the *Mavica*, at the Photokina in Germany. Canon soon followed with a still video camera called the RC-701. An experimental version was tested in practice during the Los Angeles Olympic Games in 1984. In May 1986 Canon announced it as a commercial product, and with that it became the first such camera actually being sold. Sony began marketing the Mavica camera in October 1987. Kodak followed with a prototype still video camera in the first half of 1988.

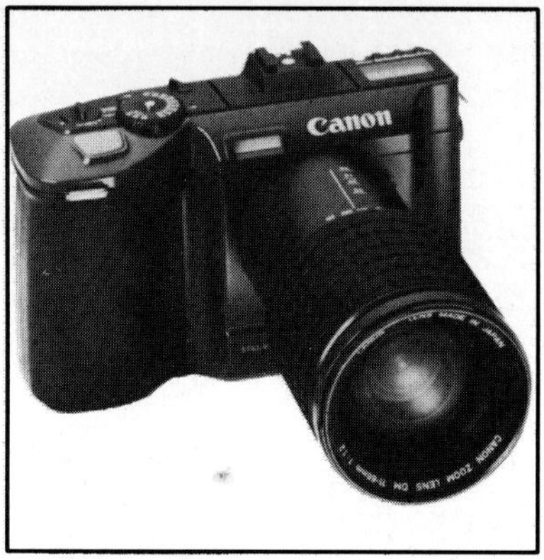

The Canon RC-701

Shown above is a picture of Canon's RC-701 camera. It looks like a normal SLR photo camera, it has all the same controls, but it takes photos on a floppy disk instead of on a film. All main companies are working on a line of products to support the new still video imaging systems. Canon, Sony, and Kodak all have developed still video recorders and players that accept the new photo floppy disks. All three companies also have developed still video image printer systems for producing hardcopy output.

The floppy disk format for the still video cameras has been standardized among the major companies. The roll-film of the future is a small 2×2 inch floppy disk that can store up to 50 color photos. To ease the transfer of images to and from video recorders, the photos are stored in video format, not in digital form. An immediate consequence of this choice is that the resolution of the still video cameras is rather crude. The CCD image sensor in the cameras is capable of recording approximately 780×490 dots per image. The effective resolution of a video image, however, is typically not higher than 480 dots per line and 480 lines per image. To make matters worse, the Canon still video camera records only one of the two "fields" that make up a video frame, e.g., only the odd-numbered lines of the picture. This reduces the effective resolution of the pictures to about 480×240 dots per image. The Kodak prototype camera and the Sony Mavica camera do not have this restriction, but also the resolution of a full video frame is still a far cry from the roughly 4000×3000 dots of a conventional film.

The reason for this poor resolution is clearly not in the cameras but in the recording format chosen and its origin in video technology. To compete with conventional films the resolution of the new cameras will have to get at least 5 times higher, and the price will have to get at least that much lower. There is, however, reason to believe that this can and will happen. One possibility is that the next generation of digital cameras will use truly digital storage of data on miniature floppy disks that can be read directly by a personal computer. The other possibility is the adoption, at least for digital photography, of the new high-definition television standard (HDTV) that has, quite independently, also been in preparation for several years. The HDTV standard would double the resolution of television and video images. Below we will talk a little more about the type of equipment that is available for digital photography right now.

Scanners and Digitizers

The simplest method to digitize a photograph is to send it to a graphics lab that has good scanning equipment. For a modest fee, say between $10 and $15, they will digitize a print or a slide and provide you with a floppy disk or a computer tape in the format you specify.

Another possibility is to buy a graphics board for the specific personal computer that you own (e.g., one of the TARGA boards for the AT&T personal computers). Most graphics boards have a *frame-grabbing* capability, that is, they have a video input port that allows you to digitize video frames directly from a video recorder or video camera. The resolution will be lower than what you can get from a good scanner, but the convenience of having your own digitizer on line will be a definite plus.

By far the best method is, of course, to purchase your own *photo-scanner* or *digitizer*. For not too much money you can buy small, low-resolution scanners that connect directly to a personal computer. They are advertised in many popular journals, such as *Byte* magazine. Commercially available high-resolution scanners range in price from a few hundred to a few hundred thousand dollars. As can be expected, the more money you spend, the better scanner you can buy. A good scanner that connects to an IBM PC or an Apple Macintosh, for instance, is the SpectraFax 200, made by the SpectraFax Corporation, in Naples, Florida. The scanner can digitize 8×10 inch color prints at 200 dots per inch, and costs about $4000.

The scanner that was used to digitize photos for this book costs about $30,000. It can scan both opaque and transparent images (i.e., both prints and negatives) at up to 750 dots per inch (8 bits per dot) over an image area of maximally 8×10 inches. It is sold by Imagitex Inc., in Nashua, New Hampshire.

Most digitizers of this type hold a single array of photo cells or CCD elements that can be moved mechanically along the length of a picture. Line by line the picture can then be scanned, with a resolution that is determined by the number of cells in the array. The electrical characteristics of the photo cell change under the influence of the light that falls on it. The scanner obtains a reading from each cell in the array that corresponds to the brightness of the image at the precise spot within the image that was focused on the cell. The cheaper scanners have fewer cells in the array and a smaller range of brightness values that can be distinguished. We will come back to the effect of this on image quality in Chapter 3. Be warned, though, that if you want to be able to process images of acceptable quality you need a system that can produce 512×512 dots (pixels) or more, with at least 8 bits per dot for black-and-white images, and at least 24 bits per dot for color images (8 bits each for red, green, and blue).

Video Printers and Film Printers

After you have scanned in the image and processed it in the digital darkroom that lives in your home computer, the image must somehow be put back on film or paper. The cheapest solution is simply to snap a picture from the monitor of your system with a Polaroid camera, but you are not likely to be satisfied for long with the quality of such prints.

A good solution is again to send a floppy disk or a tape with the digital output to a graphics labs and have them produce a high-quality image with good equipment. The graphics lab in this case performs the function of the camera store where you would go with a conventional film to have prints made. The problem for the time being is that there are not many graphics labs that process digital images. But that may change.

An alternative is to use a still video image printer that will allow you to produce a medium-resolution print of any video image. Still video image printers are sold by Sony, Kodak, and Canon. The price is around $4000 for the printer and about $1 per print made.

The best, but also the most expensive, solution is to buy your own high-resolution digital film printer that allows you to write back images onto either Polaroid film or 35mm negatives. A digital film printer reads the encoded image and varies the brightness of a light beam that writes the picture back to film in accordance with the processed information stored in the computer. As with scanners, there are cheap solutions that work slowly, at low resolution or with only a few brightness values that can be written back to film, and there are expensive solutions that can work miracles. The most expensive film printers, such as the ones used to make animation movies at the Disney Studios, can cost up to half a million dollars. The one that was used to prepare this book is the QCR D4/2 system made by Matrix Instruments Inc. in Orangeburg, New York. It has a maximum resolution of 4096×4096 dots with a brightness range from 0 to 255. It is relatively slow: it takes about 20 minutes to put a color image back on film at full resolution. Compared to its (up to 50 times) faster brothers it is also relatively cheap. It costs about $20,000.

Further Reading

A gentle and readable introduction to image processing, including an overview of the early work done at NASA's Jet Propulsion Lab in Pasadena, can be found in the March 1987 special issue of *Byte* magazine. The more theoretically inclined will probably find more than they bargain for in the following books:

Digital Image Processing, by William K. Pratt, John Wiley & Sons, New York, 1978, 750 pgs., ISBN 0-471-01888-0.

Digital Image Processing, by R. C. Gonzalez and P. A. Wintz, Addison-Wesley, Reading, Mass., 1977, 431 pgs., ISBN 0-201-02596-5.

Digital Filters — Theory and Applications, N. K. Bose, Elsevier Science Publishing Co., New York, 1985, 496 pgs., ISBN 0-444-00980-9.

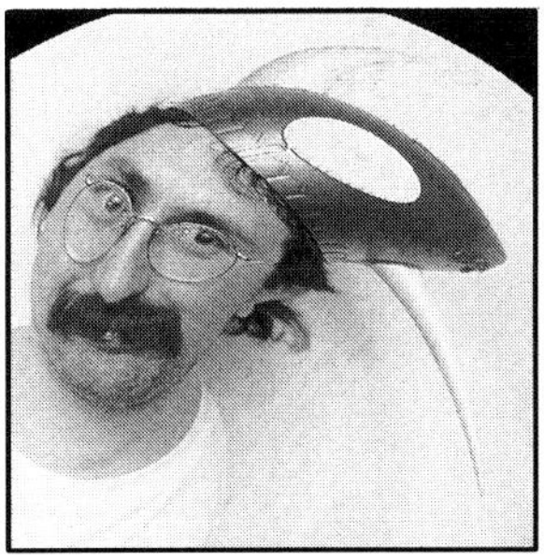

3 The Digital Darkroom

Computers work with numbers, not pictures. To get a computer to work on a picture we have to find a way to represent the image in numbers. Fortunately, the first thing that comes to mind turns out to be perfectly workable: think of the picture as a big array of dots and assign a value to each dot to represent its brightness. We will stick to black-and-white images here. For color images the same principles apply. We would use three brightness values per dot: one for each of the primary colors red, green, and blue. Two questions that remain are: How many dots (*pixels*) do we need, and how large a value should be used to define each dot?

From Pictures to Numbers

Let's start with the basics. Photographic film, say 35mm black-and-white film, has an exposure range in the order of 1:256 and a resolving power of roughly 4000 dots per inch. For photographic paper the numbers are somewhat lower, on the order of 1000 dots per inch resolution and a brightness range of 1:30, but for now let us use the quality of the film storing the original image as a reference. To store a brightness value between 0 and 255 we need an 8-bit number (2^8 equals 256), quite happily the size of a byte on most machines. So, one part of the problem is easily solved: each dot in the image to be digitized can be stored in one byte of memory. One frame on a 35mm film measures 24×36mm or roughly 0.9×1.4 inches. If we digitize the frame at 4000 dots per inch, each frame will produce 0.9×4000×1.4×4000 numbers, which corresponds to some 20 megabytes of data. But this is only part of the story.

The negative holds enough information to allow us to make enlargements on photographic paper at an acceptable resolution. If we enlarge the 24×36mm frame five times, the effective resolution of the enlargement drops from 4000 dots per inch on the film to 800 dots per inch on the print. Another reference is the resolving power of the eye. After all, the image only needs to have a certain resolution to make the dots invisible to the eye. How many dots can we distinguish on a print? The resolving power of a human eye is approximately 1/60 of a degree, which means that even under optimal conditions we cannot resolve more than about 600 dots per inch at a viewing distance of 12 inches. An image digitized and reproduced at 600 dots per inch is indistinguishable from the original under normal viewing conditions. Most of the photos in this book were digitized at 750 dots per inch. Just for comparison, the resolution of a television image is less than 500 by 500 dots, which on a 15 inch diagonal screen corresponds to about 47 dots per inch.

Z Is for White

To make it easier to talk about digitized images and image transformations, we will introduce some shorthand. Let's stick to the analogy of a picture as a two-dimensional array of dots. Each dot then has three attributes: one number defining its brightness and two other numbers defining its location in the array (and in the image). Since we will use these three numbers quite extensively, I will give them names. There is nothing special about these names: they are just shorthand. The two numbers defining the location of a dot within a picture will be named `x` and `y` and the brightness of the dot can be called `z`.

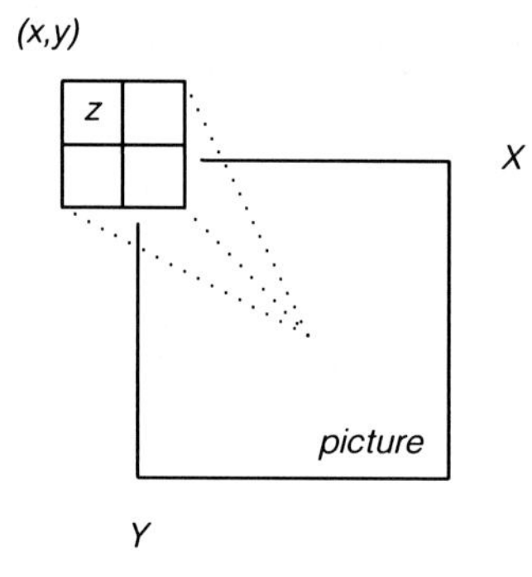

The Sampling Grid

The dots are really "samples" of the brightness in the real image. The `(x,y)` grid is therefore sometimes referred to as the "sampling grid."

For a given picture the `x`, `y`, and `z` are of course not independent. Given the first two, the last one is determined: `z` is a function of `x` and `y`. The value of `z` at position `(x,y)` in some image named `picture` is written as

```
picture[x,y].
```

It is convenient to introduce symbols for the maximum values of the three numbers just named. The picture width in dots is named `X`. The `x` coordinate ranges in value from 0 to `X`−1. Similarly, `Y` is the picture *height*. The `y` coordinate ranges from 0 to `Y`−1. `Z`, finally, defines the maximum brightness value of the dots. If we use one byte per dot, `Z` will be 255, and `z` can have a value between 0 and 255. `X` and `Y` may turn out to be 512 or 1024, depending on the size of the picture and the resolution at which it was scanned, but the precise values are largely irrelevant from this point on. A low value for `z` means a low brightness (dark) and a high value is a high brightness (light). A low value for `x` refers to the left side of the image and a low value for `y` refers to the top.

A Picture Transformation Language

Given sufficient resolution, any image can be translated into numbers and those numbers can be translated back into an image. Our purpose here is to find a simple way to describe images and image transformations. To do that we are developing a little language that consists of symbols like the `x`, `y`, and `z` introduced above, and some transformation expressions. Two symbols that come in handy for defining transformations are `old` and `new`. We use the first to refer to the result of the last transformation performed. The second symbol, `new`, refers to the destination of the current transformation: the newly created image. We can also refer to specific dots in the old or new image by writing `old[x,y]` and `new[x,y]`, where `x` and `y` are as defined above. So, using only the symbols introduced so far, we can *create* a picture by writing in this language:

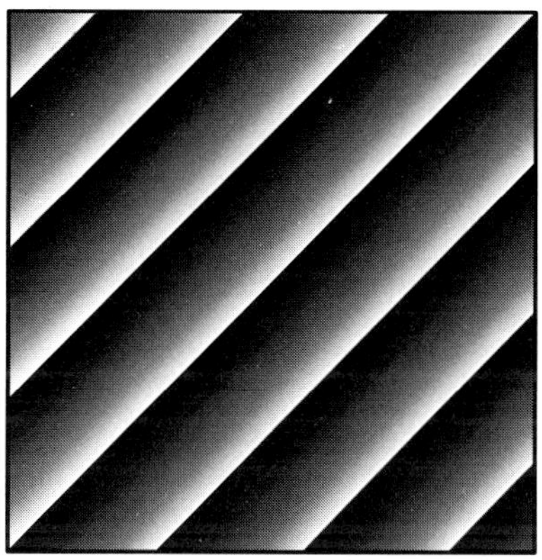

`new[x,y] = x+y` *(3.1)*

The expression defines a brightness `x+y` of the image `new` for each dot at position `(x,y)`. It may confuse you that a location is translated into a brightness, but that's exactly what we are doing! The expression `x+y` produces a number and all numbers together define an image. But there's a catch. The brightness value of the dots in the `new` image is restricted to values between 0 and `Z`, but the maximum value of `x+y` can of course be much larger than `Z`. If dots are stored in bytes, the values assigned will wrap around the maximum value `Z`. If we want we can make this effect explicit by using *modulo* arithmetic. If `x+y` ⩾ `Z+1`, we subtract `Z+1` as often as necessary from `x+y` to get a value that fits the range. So, a brightness value `Z` remains `Z`, but `Z+1` becomes 0, and 3*Z+12 becomes 9. The value of an expression E taken modulo-Z is usually written as E%Z. As a variation on (3.1) we can try:

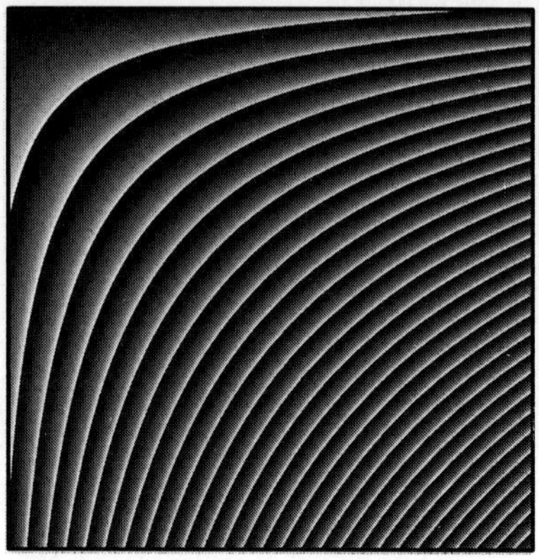

(3.2)

(3.3)

```
new[x,y] = (x*y)%(Z+1)
```
(3.2)

The modulo operator % will come back a few more times below. For now, just remember that all brightness values are by default modulo Z+1. The range of available brightness values can be matched precisely to the grid:

```
new[x,y] = (Z*x*y)/((X-1)*(Y-1))
```
(3.3)

In the upper left-hand corner both x and y are zero and thus the brightness z at new[0,0] will be zero, or solidly black. In the lower right-hand corner x*y=(X-1)*(Y-1) and z reaches its maximum value Z: white.

But why do only things that make sense? We just talked about the modulo operator %, so let's try something like

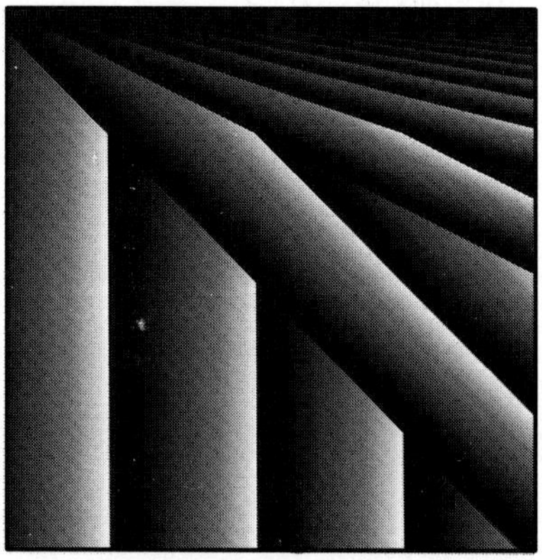

```
new[x,y] = x%y
```
(3.4)

Where x is smaller than y (the lower left triangle) the picture could as well have been defined as `new[x,y]=x`, which, since dots are stored in bytes, is interpreted as `new[x,y]=x%(Z+1)`. Note that you can tell from the picture what the current values for `X` and `Y` are, given that `Z=255`.

Trigonometry Made Pretty

If we also include trigonometric functions in our picture language, we can really start experimenting. Let `sin(a)` be the sine function that returns a value between +1.0 and −1.0. Its argument `a` is an angle given in degrees. Try to explain the patterns defined by

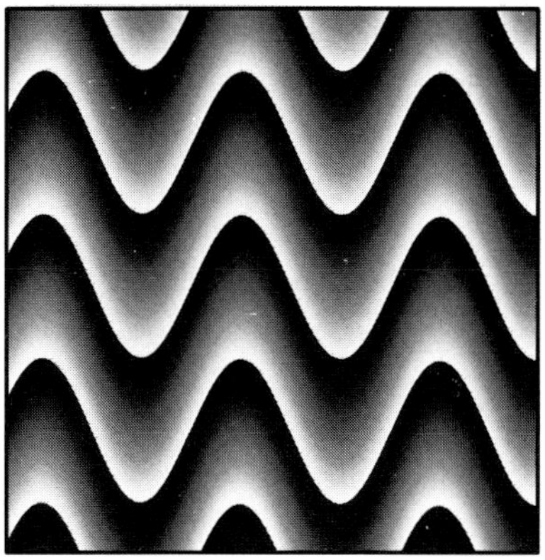

(3.5)

(3.6)

```
new[x,y] = y+(sin(x)*Z)/2                    (3.5)
```

and, with `atan(y,x)` returning the arc-tangent of `y/x` in degrees,

```
new[x,y] = (atan(y-Y/2,x-X/2)*Z)/360         (3.6)
```

The possibilities for creating intricate patterns with random mathematical functions are endless. With some effort you can even find pictorial representations for interesting mathematical theorems.

Conditional Transformations

It is time to add a little more power to our expression language. We will use the notation

```
(condition)?yes:no
```

to mean that if the `condition` is true (or nonzero), the transformation is defined by expression `yes`, otherwise it is defined by `no`. So, trivially,

```
new[x,y] = (0)?Z:0                           (3.7)
```

defines an all-black image, and

```
new[x,y] = (Z>0)?old[x,y]:0                  (3.8)
```

has no effect whatsoever (the condition always holds). Note also that "transformation" (3.7) is independent of `x` and `y` coordinates: it defines the same new brightness value `Z` for every dot in the image, independent of its location.

Between the lines you have already been sold on the idea that an image (`old`) can be used in a transformation just as easily as an expression. We will explore this in more detail in the section titled *Geometric Transformations*.

Using the modulo operator and conditional transformations, we can define interesting patterns with one-liners such as the following two.

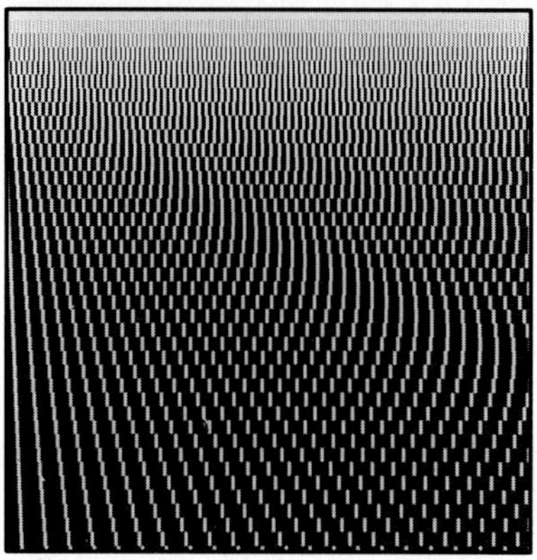

(3.9)

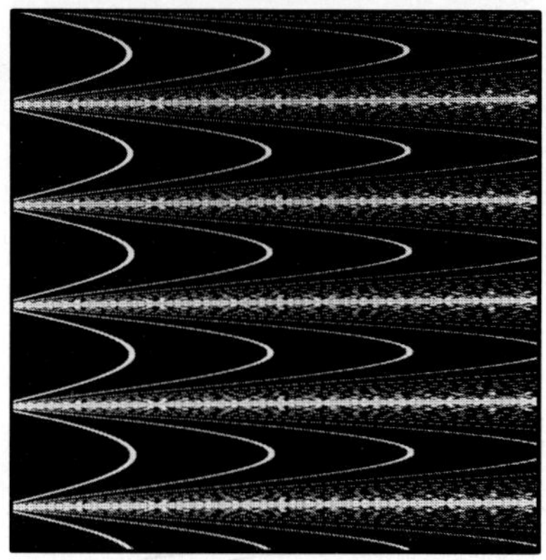

(3.10)

```
new[x,y] = ((x%(5+y/25))>5)?0:Z          (3.9)
new[x,y] = (Z*abs(x%sin(y))>10)?0:Z     (3.10)
```

There is again an infinite number of variations on this theme. We can, for instance, try to make a composite of two photos, using some mathematical function, or even the brightness of a third photo in the conditional.

Polar Coordinates

Now let us slightly change the rules of this game. All expressions that we have invented so far used the symbols `x` and `y`. The `x` and the `y` were defined as Cartesian coordinates in the image array. We can also consider the image area as a simple two-dimensional plane with an arbitrary coordinate system for locating the individual dots.

We can, for instance, define a *polar* coordinate system, with the origin in the middle, and again two numbers to find the location of dots relative to the origin. We name the polar coordinates `r` and `a`. The radius `r` is the distance of a dot from the origin, and `a` is the angle between a line from the dot to the origin and a fixed, but otherwise arbitrary, line through the origin.

Cartesian Coordinates

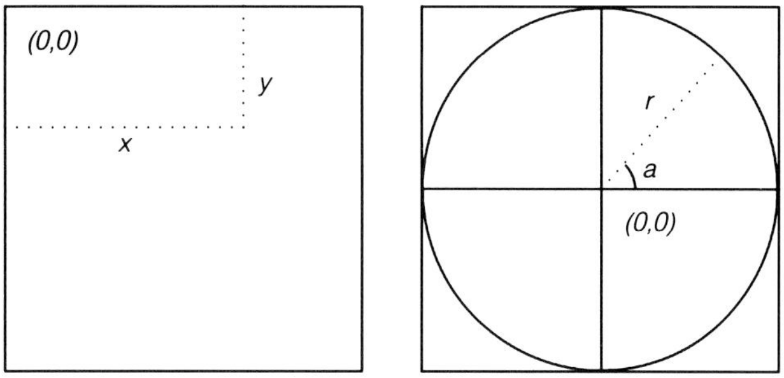

Polar Coordinates

We can again introduce a special shorthand **R** for the maximum radius and a shorthand **A** for the maximum angle (360°). The origin of the polar coordinate system is `(X/2,Y/2)` in Cartesian coordinates, and similarly, the origin of the Cartesian coordinate system is `(R,3*A/8)` in polar coordinates.

Now it is easy to make the picture

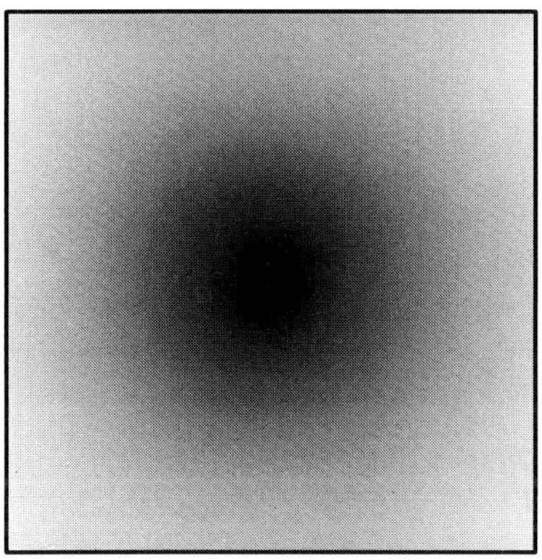

(3.11)

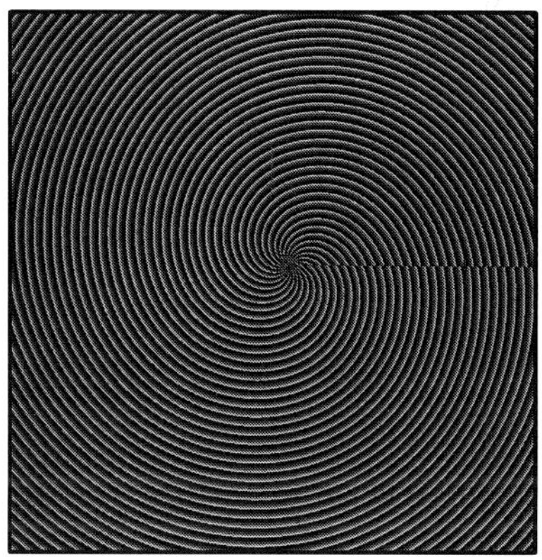

(3.12)

```
new[r,a] = (Z*r)/R                              (3.11)
```

or the more inspiring

```
new[r,a] = (((a+r)%16)-8)*Z/16+Z/2              (3.12)
```

But enough said about these artificial images. The expressions that we used to calculate brightness values above can also be used to calculate a malicious deformation of an existing image: It's time to try our hand at some real image transformations.

Point Processes

Image transformations come in a number of flavors. We can, for instance, distinguish between point processes, area processes, and frame processes. A transformation that assigns new brightness values to individual dots, using only the old brightness value of a dot, is called a *point process.* A simple point process is

```
new[x,y] = Z-old[x,y]                                  (3.13)
```

which makes a negative by subtracting each dot from the maximum brightness value Z. Another example is

```
new[x,y] = Z*log(old[x,y])/log(Z)                      (3.14)
```

This particular transformation can be used as part of a correction filter to cope with the "nonlinearity" of devices such as scanners and display monitors: the tendency to lose detail in the dark areas of the picture. The above transformation corrects for nonlinearity by boosting the values of the darker pixels with a logarithmic function.

We can also simulate the effect of photographic "solarization" with a point process. The solarization effect was discovered by Armand Sabattier in 1860. If, in a conventional darkroom, a partly developed image is exposed to raw light, the previously unexposed areas turn from positive to negative, but the previously exposed areas remain as they are. We can simulate this effect with the following transformation, applied here to a portrait of Jim McKie.

```
new[x,y] = (old[x,y]<Z/2)?Z-old[x,y]:old[x,y]          (3.15)
```

We can also slowly fade in a solarization effect from left to right, for instance with:

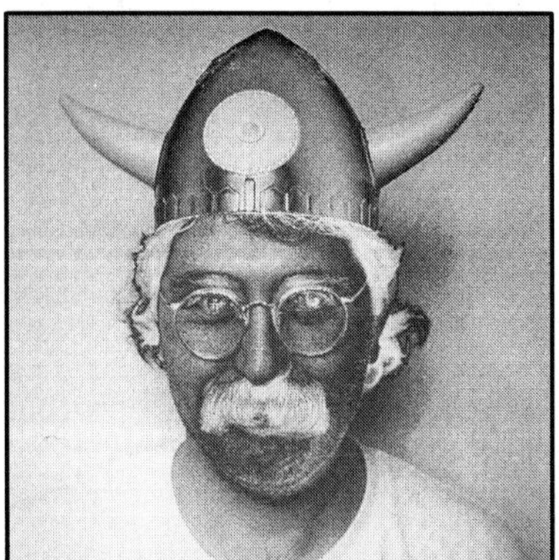

(3.15)

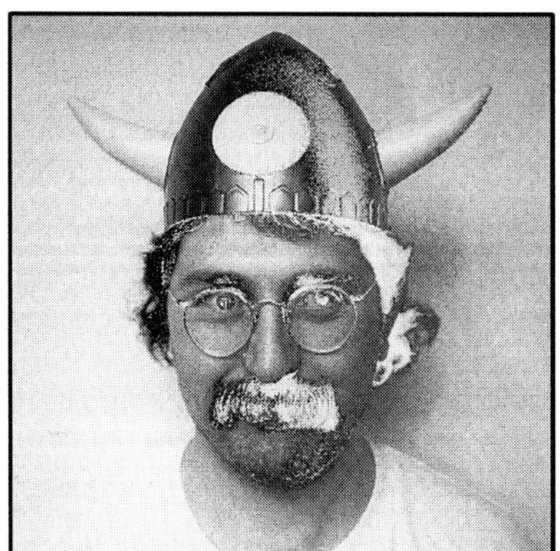

(3.16)

```
new[x,y] =
(old[x,y]>(Z*x)/(2*X))?old[x,y]:Z-old[x,y]             (3.16)
```

Or we could use the brightness values of one portrait to solarize another. A point process can also be used to enhance or reduce contrast in a photo. Using conditional expressions we can also apply these changes to only specific parts of a picture.

Area Processes

If not just the old brightness value of the dot itself is used, but values of the dots in a small area around it, the point process becomes an *area process*. An image can be blurred a little by calculating the average brightness value of each dot and four of its neighbors.

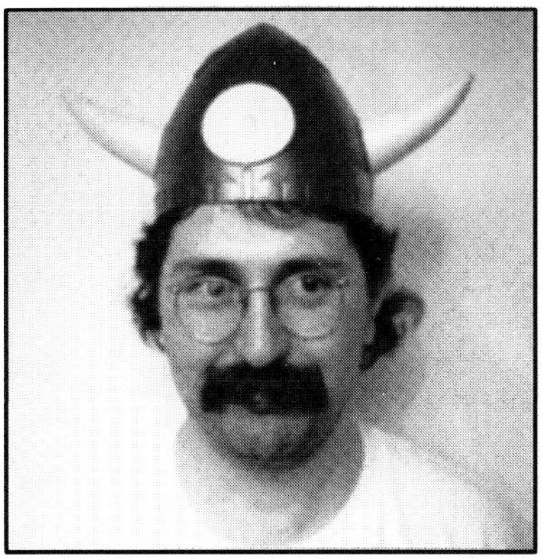

(3.17)

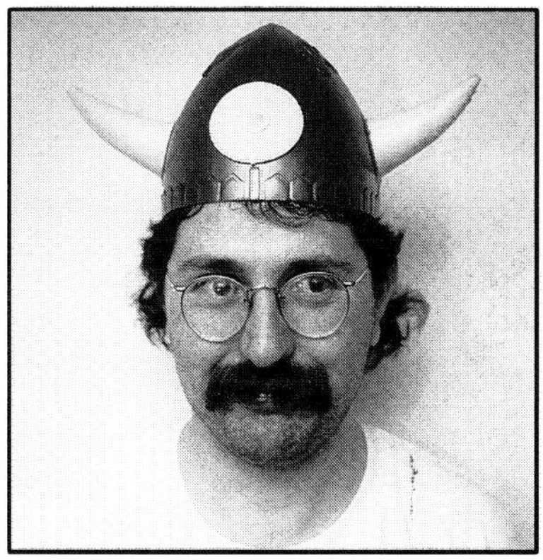

(3.18)

```
new[x,y] = (old[x,y]+
old[x-1,y]+old[x+1,y]+old[x,y-1]+old[x,y+1])/5
```
(3.17)

The blurring can be applied to a larger area surrounding each pixel (as shown in Chapter 6) to enhance the effect. Or, using polar coordinates, the amount of blurring can be varied with the radius to simulate the soft-focus effect of an old lens.

If we can blur an image by *adding* neighboring dots to each pixel and normalizing, imagine what would happen if we *subtract* the brightness values of neighboring dots from each pixel. With the right normalization again we can write this as follows.

```
new[x,y] = 5*old[x,y]-
old[x-1,y]-old[x+1,y]-old[x,y-1]-old[x,y+1]
```
(3.18)

The effect of the transformation is a digital filtering that works as though it restored the focus in a blurry image. Formally, the process approximates the working of a *Laplacian* filter ∇^2.

Another example of an area process is this one to make a relief. The transformation is useful in more serious image processing applications as a fast edge detection filter, illustrated here with a portrait of Brian Redman.

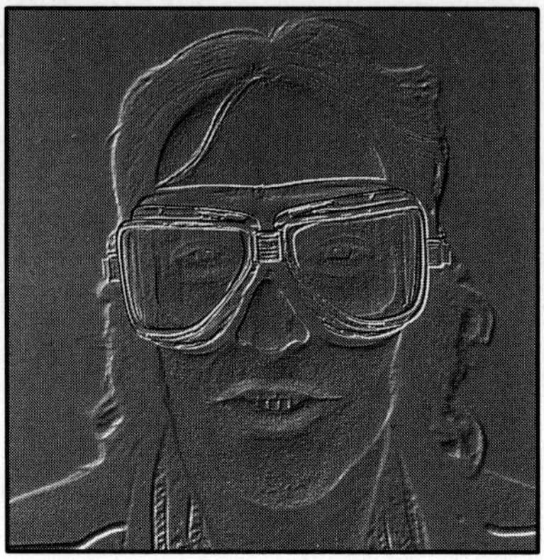

```
new[x,y] = old[x,y]+(Z/2-old[x+2,y+2])
```
(3.19)

Geometric Transformations

With a third type of transformation we can define geometric transformations to the sampling grid and change the coordinates of the dots in an image. The standard mapping defines a regular grid of dots. Geometric transformations are used to reshape that grid. If the portrait of Brian Redman is stored in an array named `ber`, we can write

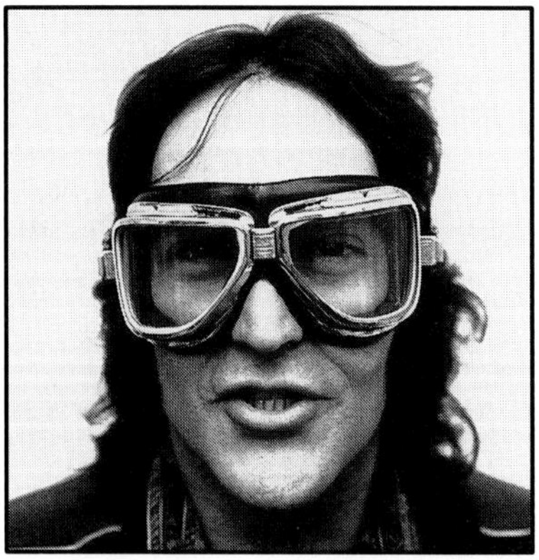

(3.20)

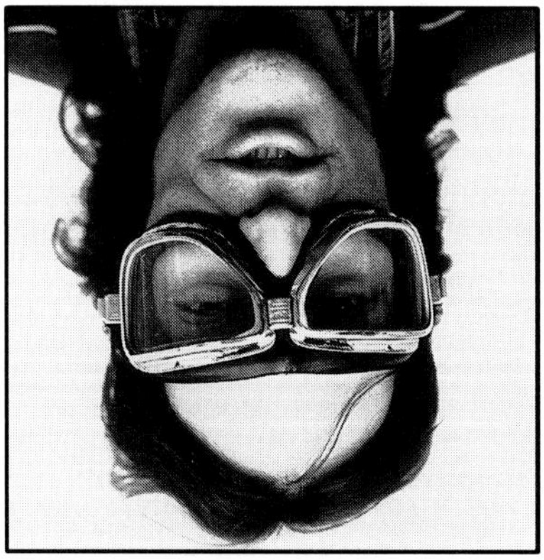

(3.21)

```
new[x,y] = ber[x,y]
```
(3.20)

which is the normal photo on the standard grid with each dot at location `(x,y)` in `ber` mapped to a new dot at precisely the same location in the `new` image. This is still a point process. But we can play more interesting games with the picture. For instance, `new[x,y] = ber[x, Y-y]` *(3.21)*

turns the picture upside down, by reversing the `y` coordinate in the grid. And, only slightly more complicated,

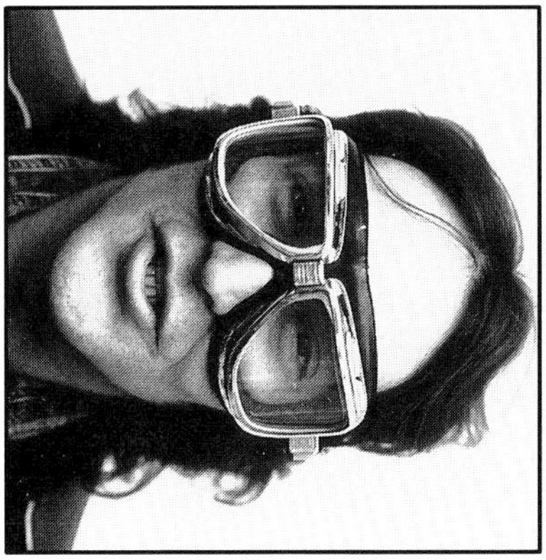

(3.22)

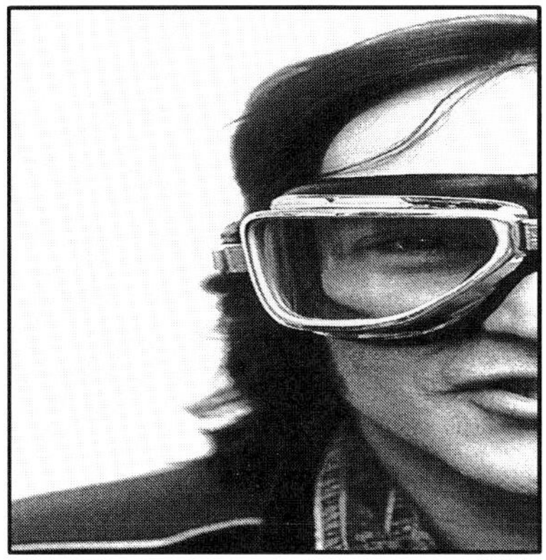

(3.23)

`new[x,y] = ber[y,X-x]` *(3.22)*

rotates the image by 90^{0} clockwise. The `x` and `y` coordinates are swapped, and the order of the `x` is reversed. Reversing the order of `y` instead of `x` makes the image rotate counterclockwise.

We are still using all the dots in the old image to create the new one. We can also break that rule and try something like

`new[x,y] = ber[x/2,y]` *(3.23)*

to stretch the image horizontally by a factor of 2. This stretching operation can be made more interesting still by using arbitrary trigonometric functions to calculate the offset, or by stretching both the `x` and `y` coordinates. Note also that

`new[x,y] = old[x*2,y*2]` *(3.24)*

is a simple way to shrink an image. However, to avoid having the coordinates overflow their maxima and cause havoc, it is more prudent to write either

`new[x,y] = old[(x*2)%(X+1),(y*2)%(Y+1)]` *(3.25)*

or

`new[x,y] = (x≤X/2&&y≤Y/2)?old[x*2,y*2]:0` *(3.26)*

The most rewarding geometric transformations on portraits are made with conditional expressions. We can, for example, make a perfect mirror composite of a portrait, once it is centered properly. These transformations

`new[x,y] = (x>=X/2)?bwk[x,y]:bwk[X-x,y]` *(3.27)*

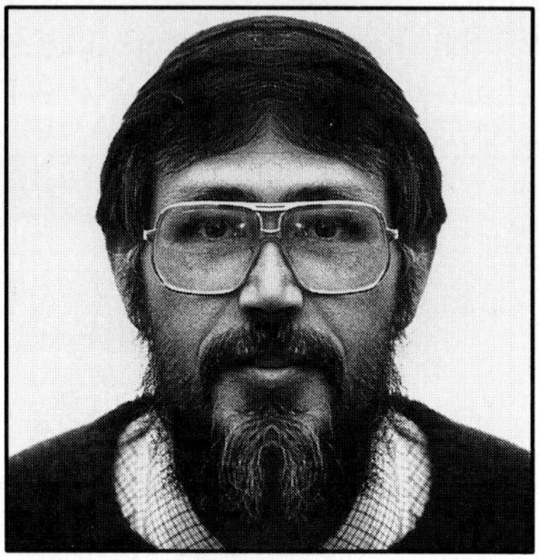

(3.27)

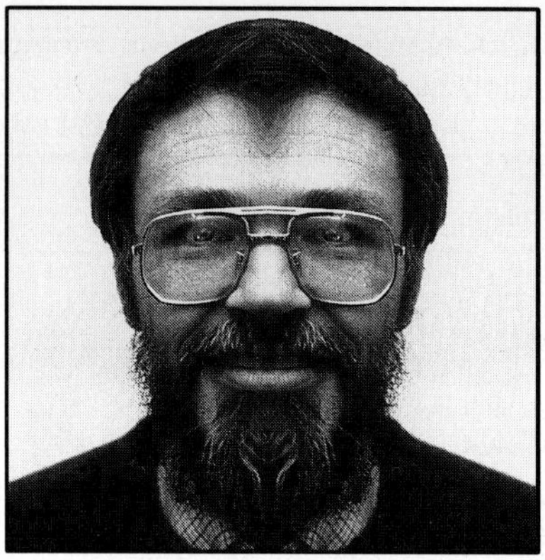

(3.28)

```
new[x,y] = (x<X/2)?bwk[x,y]:bwk[X-x,y]
```
(3.28)

are two different ways to mirror a portrait of Brian Kernighan vertically along its middle axis. Of course, even more startling effects can be produced by mirroring along a horizontal axis.

If we can do all this with a single image, imagine what could be done with two or more! Let's see how we could use the portraits of Rob Pike and Peter Weinberger. Here they are first shown in their original, unedited, version.

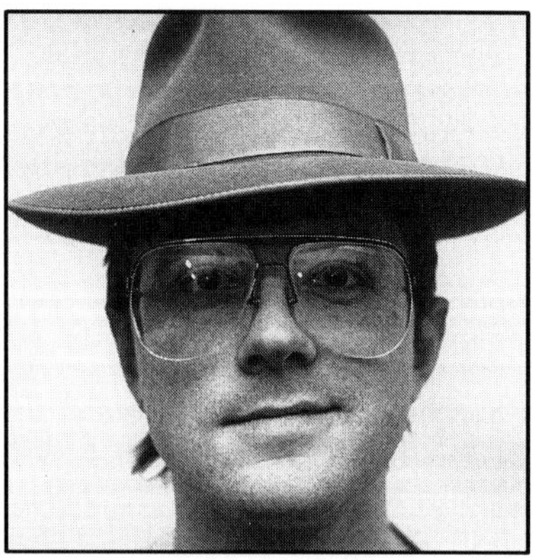

Rob Pike

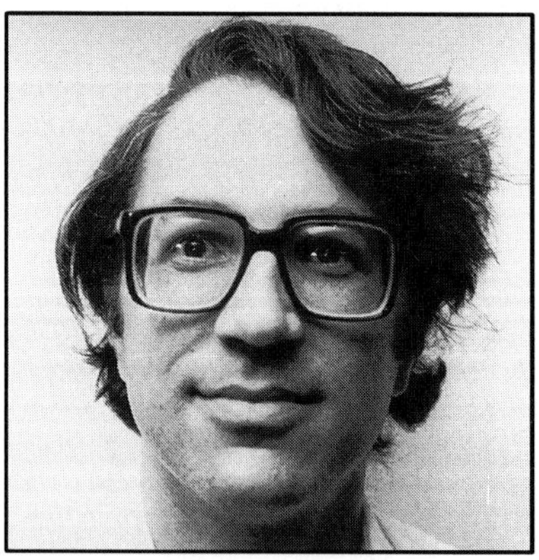

Peter Weinberger

Frame Processes

Transformations that work on multiple images are called *frame processes*. Suppose we have the portraits of Rob Pike and Peter Weinberger stored in two image files named `rob` and `pjw`. An average of the two is quickly defined, though not very inspiring.

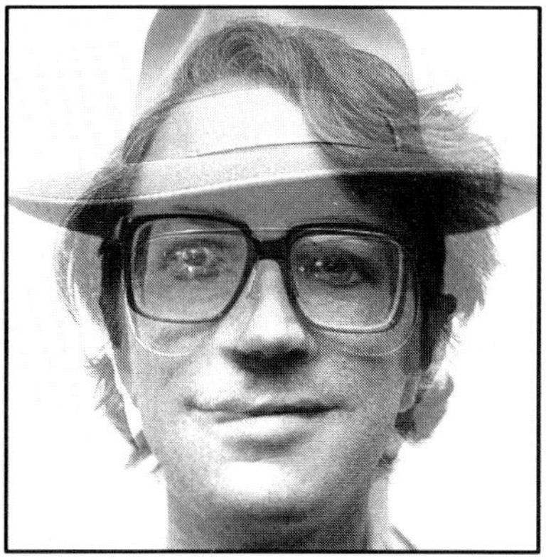

(3.29)

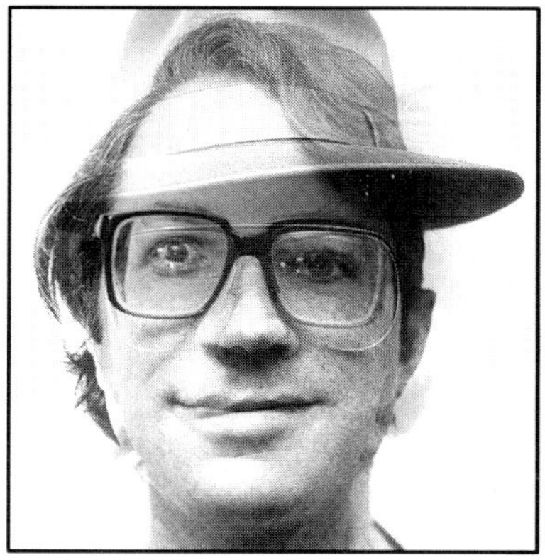

(3.30)

```
new[x,y] = (rob[x,y]+pjw[x,y])/2
```
(3.29)

All we have to do is add the pictures and divide by 2. We can also fade one picture slowly into the other, which makes for a more interesting picture. A first attempt might be a full linear fade.

```
new[x,y] = (x*rob[x,y]+(X-x)*pjw[x,y])/X
```
(3.30)

But that doesn't really work out too well. If we restrict the fade to just the middle part of the image, it looks better. The transformation expression we need must have a different effect in three different areas of the image: left, middle, and right. We can use a conditional transformation again to accomplish this, but note that we need more than one condition this time. We can do that with a nested conditional as follows.

```
(left)?pjw:(right)?rob:fade
```

The last part

```
(right)?rob:fade
```

is treated as a separate transformation expression that takes effect only when the condition `(right)` of the first expression is false. Transformation (3.31) shows the details.

```
new[x,y] = (x<X/3)?pjw:(x>2*X/3)?rob
    :((x-X/3)*rob+(2*X/3-x)*pjw)*3/X
```
(3.31)

We can also do this transformation in a vertical plane, and use two, more carefully selected, portraits, to achieve the following effect (admittedly, the resulting photo was touched up a little with a separate editor).

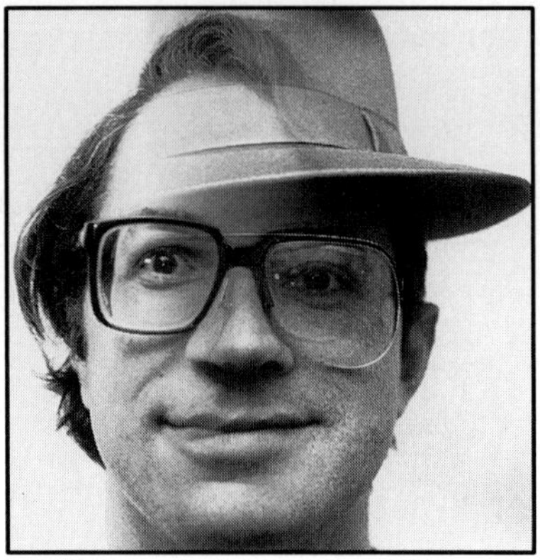

(3.31)

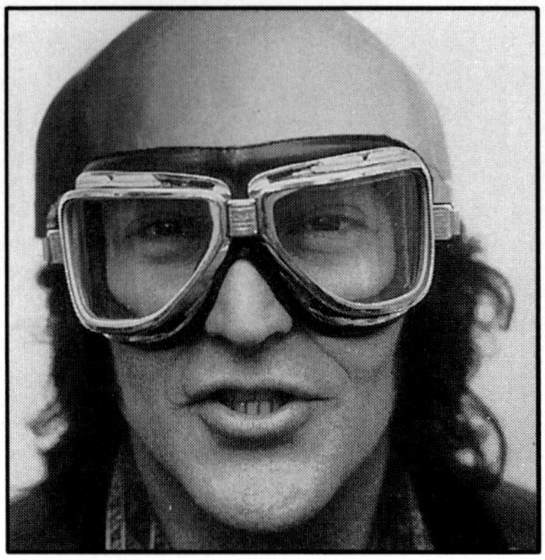

(3.32)

```
new[x,y] = (y<Y/3)?ber:(y>2*Y/3)?skull
  :((y-Y/3)*skull+(2*Y/3-y)*ber)*3/Y
```
(3.32)

Again, nothing prevents us from experimenting at length with even less useful compositions. We can, for instance, use the brightness of an image in the conditional,

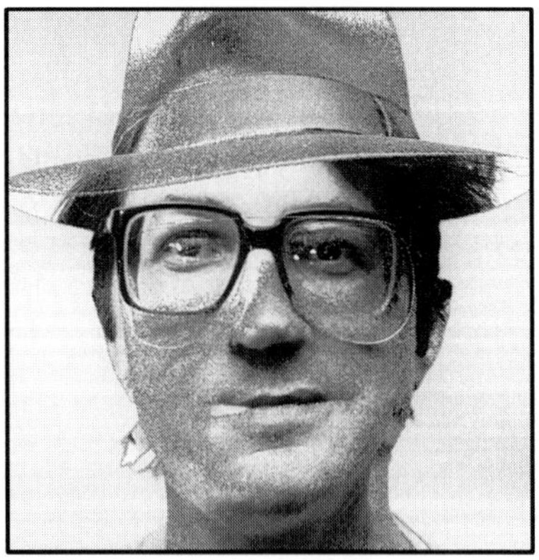

(3.33)

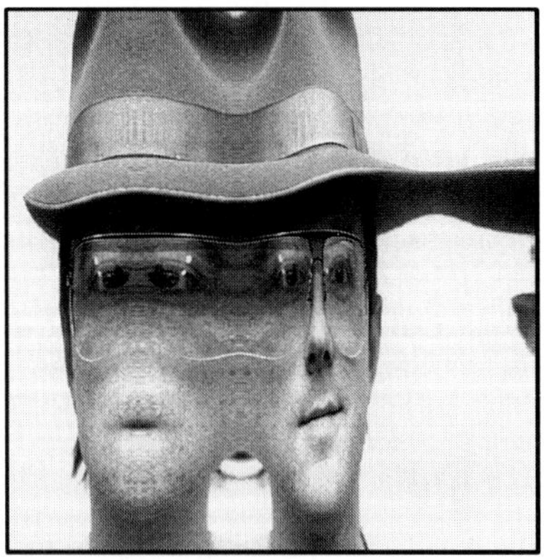

(3.34)

```
new[x,y] = (rob[x,y]>Z/2)?rob[x,y]:pjw[x,y]
```
(3.33)

or play more involved tricks with the coordinates

```
new[x,y] = rob[x+(X*cos(((x-C)*A)*2/X))/6,y]
```
(3.34)

where **A** is the maximum angle 360, and **C** is a constant. In this case **X** was

684 and c was 512.

And There's More

Well, we have now set the stage for more interesting work. What follows in Chapter 4 is a selection of the most startling image transformations we happened upon while playing with this picture language. Chapter 5 includes a discussion of some software that can be used to build an image editor to experiment further with these transformations on a home computer. Chapter 6 gives an overview of the image transformations that we have discussed.

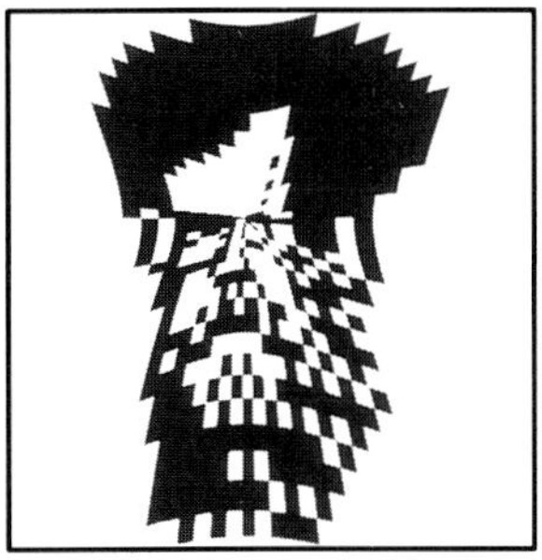

4 Altered Images

About the Photos

Somewhere toward the end of 1983 our group of about fifty researchers started using a new type of computer terminal.* Immediately, people set to work to try and exploit its graphics capabilities. Luca Cardelli (now with DEC's Systems Research Center in Palo Alto) had thought of a way to convert photos manually into little black-and-white icon bitmaps. We found a victim (a picture of computer scientist Edsger W. Dijkstra) and set to work. The process was first to reduce the photograph with a Xerox copier to a wallet-size picture of high contrast, then draw a 12×12 grid on it, make a checkerboard pattern with black-and-white squares, and then type the resulting array of dots into the computer. The result was this picture:

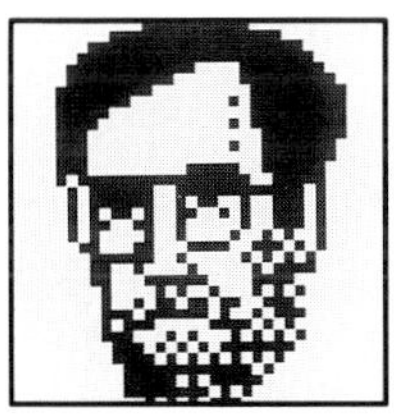

The EWD Icon

Luca made a demonstration program featuring Dijkstra's portrait as a bouncing ball. We digitized a few more portraits manually, but soon became bored

---

* The *blit* terminal was developed jointly by Bart Locanthi and Rob Pike. It was built and marketed by Teletype as the DMD 5620. The acronym DMD stands for "dot mapped display."

with the process.

Someone then came up with the idea to make a new mail server that would announce the arrival of computer mail on our terminals by showing a little portrait of the sender. Luca Cardelli wrote a first version called *vismon* (a pun on an existing program called *sysmon*). Rob Pike talked us all into posing for 4×5 inch Polaroid portraits. Not knowing what they were in for, everybody, from secretary to executive director, cooperated with the picture project. The pictures were digitized with a scanner borrowed from our image processing colleagues. Within a few days we thus obtained close to 100 portraits that have become a main source for image processing experiments.

The next step in this sequence was when Rob Pike and Dave Presotto developed the software for a centralized data base of portraits. They called it the *face server*. The *vismon* program was rewritten to use the face server. Ever since then *vismon* has been one of the most popular programs on our computers.

The face server is used both by the mail program to announce computer mail and by a printer spooler to identify the owner of jobs send to our laser printers. The picture below shows an afternoon's worth of mail from vismon: a police lineup of digitized faces. The bar on the left is a remnant of the original program *sysmon*. It shows the load on the computer system itself.

Vismon Display

Including the portrait of new colleagues into the face server's data base is now a routine operation. A photo is digitized into 512×512 dots, then halftoned and converted into a 48×48 bit icon with a program called *mugs* written by Tom Duff. The icon is then included in the data base maintained by the face server.

As a side effect from the effort to build the face server we had suddenly obtained a data base of digitized portraits, just begging to be used for purposes other than the mere announcement of computer mail. Although my main research is not in computer graphics, I could not resist the temptation to write a program called *zunk* with which I could swap eyes and noses in portraits.

I quickly found out that people can be remarkably creative when it comes to altering portraits of colleagues. Since *zunk* was not a true picture editor I ended up adding special-purpose portions to the program for each new mean transformation that we thought of. When the number of *zunk* options was over 50 I opted for a different strategy. The language for picture transformations, shown in Chapter 3, solved the problem and together with Rob Pike and Ken Thompson I built a picture editor called *pico* that is responsible for most of the pictures that follow. The editor itself was built in only a few weeks of frantic work. Over the years it has grown quite a bit. The language of the current version of *pico* is much richer than what we have shown so far. Special-purpose software was also added to support monitors for the real-time display of image transforms. But the basic structure and elegance of the editor has been maintained, and *pico* has proven to be an irresistible toy.

The pages that follow can be read as a *cookbook* of image transformations. Each recipe in this sequence takes two pages. The left page will show the original image with an explanation of the specific transformation used, and perhaps some intermediate images that were needed to create the final version. The right-hand page will show the finished image. Naturally, since most of the pictures in our data base are from colleagues, they will be featured most prominently here. Most transformations, however, can be applied to any image whatsoever. And you do not even have to be very precise when you try to duplicate the effects. One of the nicest things about image transformations of this type is that the result of typos and even of utter mistakes can still be quite fascinating and more often than not lead to solid improvements.

1

The original for the first picture is a portrait of Albert Einstein, taken by Philippe Halsman in 1947. The unedited version is shown below. The photo was scanned at a resolution of 2048×2048 pixels and transformed with the following expression, using polar instead of Cartesian coordinates:

```
new[r,a] = einstein[sqrt(r*R), a]
```

The effect is that the image shrinks toward the center. You can think of it as a projection of the image onto a cone, with the tip of the cone in the middle of the picture.

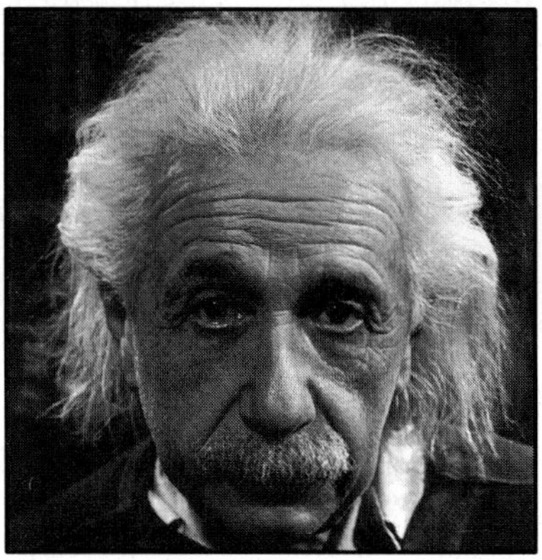

Photograph by Philippe Halsman, © Yvonne Halsmann.

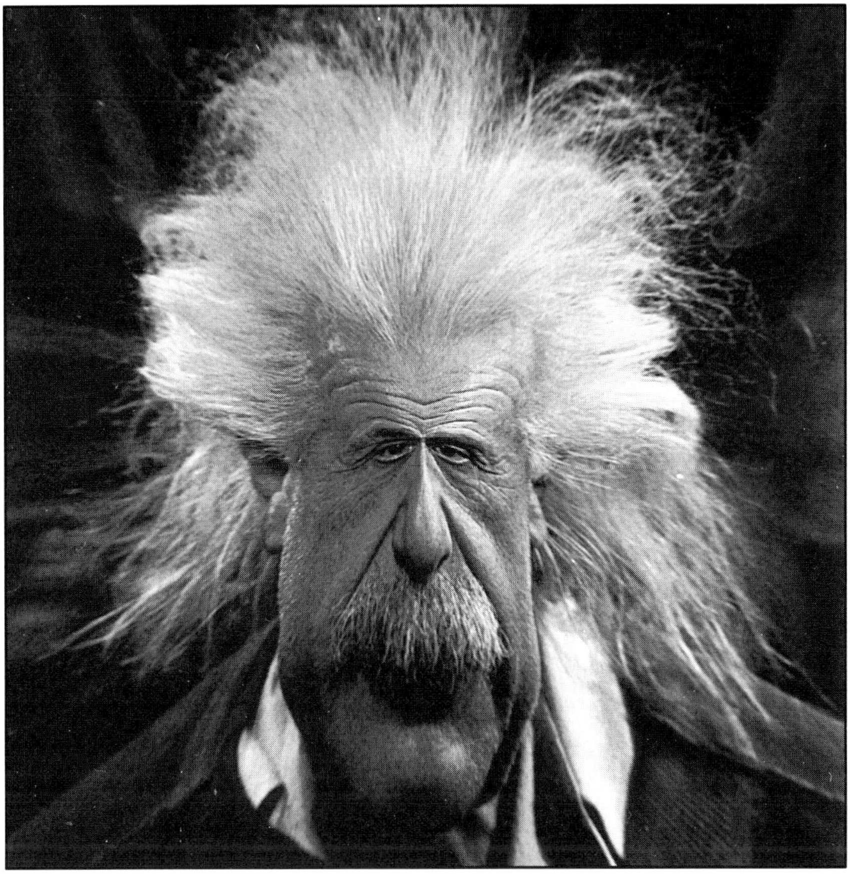

Einstein Caricature

2

For the next transformation we use a classic portrait of Alexander Graham Bell, taken by a photographer named Holton in 1876. This strange variant of the portrait was created by randomly moving rows in the picture array left and right and by moving columns up and down. The difference in shift between two adjacent columns or two adjacent rows is never more than one dot. The transformation function is given in Chapter **6**.

The original portrait is shown below.

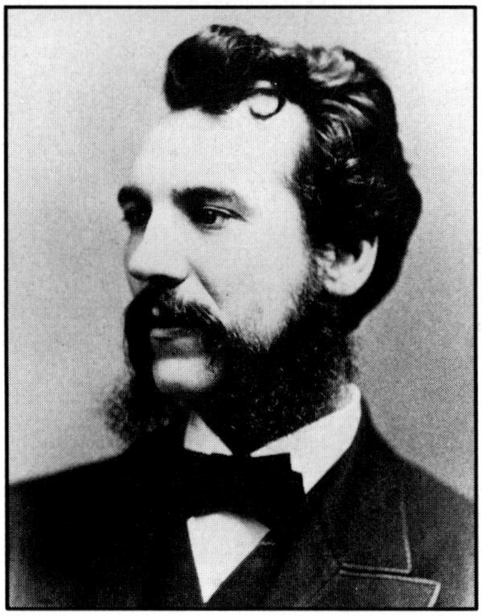

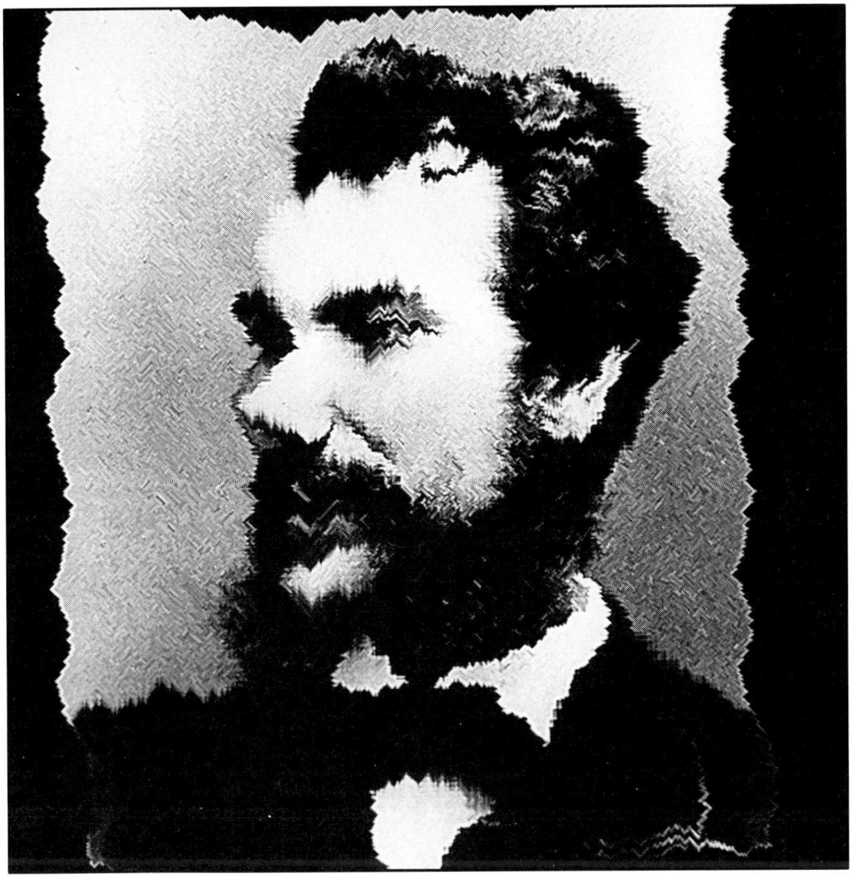

Bell Shear

3

The photo on the right is a striking example of how subtle, quite involved, picture editing operations can be performed at high resolution. No airbrush was used, no paint was needed to cover up anything in this picture. The photo is a composite of the face of Robert Oppenheimer and the hair of Albert Einstein. The two portraits were first lined up and averaged, as in

```
new[x,y] = (ein[X-x,y]+opp[x,y])/2
```

The picture of Einstein is mirrored to match the direction of light in the other portrait. I indicated with a rough line where the transition between the two pictures should take place. Using this line I made a *matte*: a separate picture that is black where one picture is supposed to be and white everywhere else. The edge from black to white was then blurred, again by computer (Chapter 3, equation *3.17*), into a soft slope of gray values to make the transition less abrupt. The final picture was a simple addition of the two portraits, using the matte to decide how much of each picture should be visible at each dot:

```
new[x,y] = matte[x,y]*ein[X-x,y]+(Z-matte[x,y])*opp[x,y]
```

The whole operation took less then an hour of my time, and mere seconds of the computer's. The originals of the two portraits are shown below. A routine for extracting an image matte from a picture is given in Chapter 6.

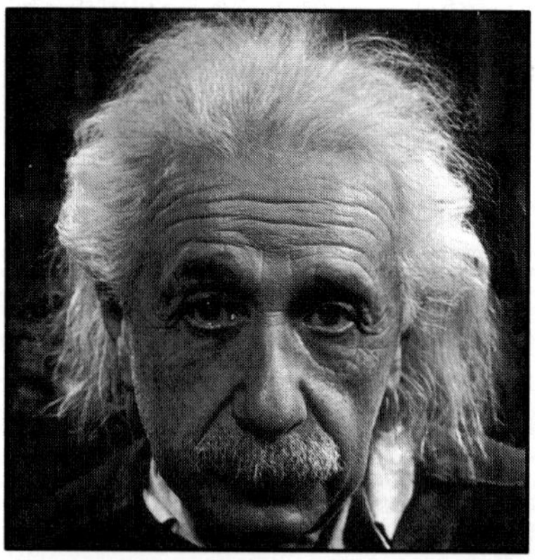

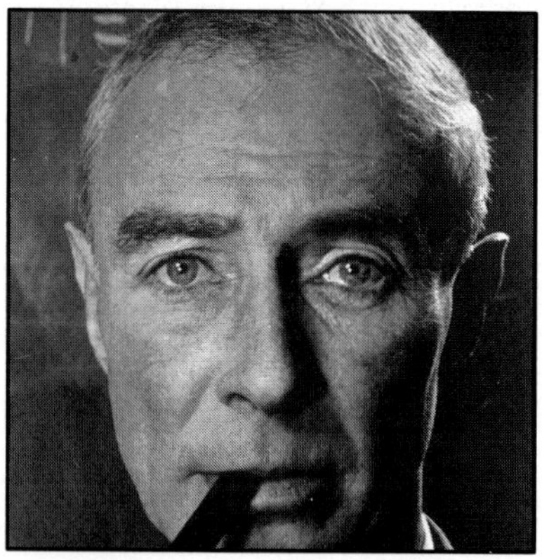

Both photographs by Philippe Halsman, © Yvonne Halsmann.

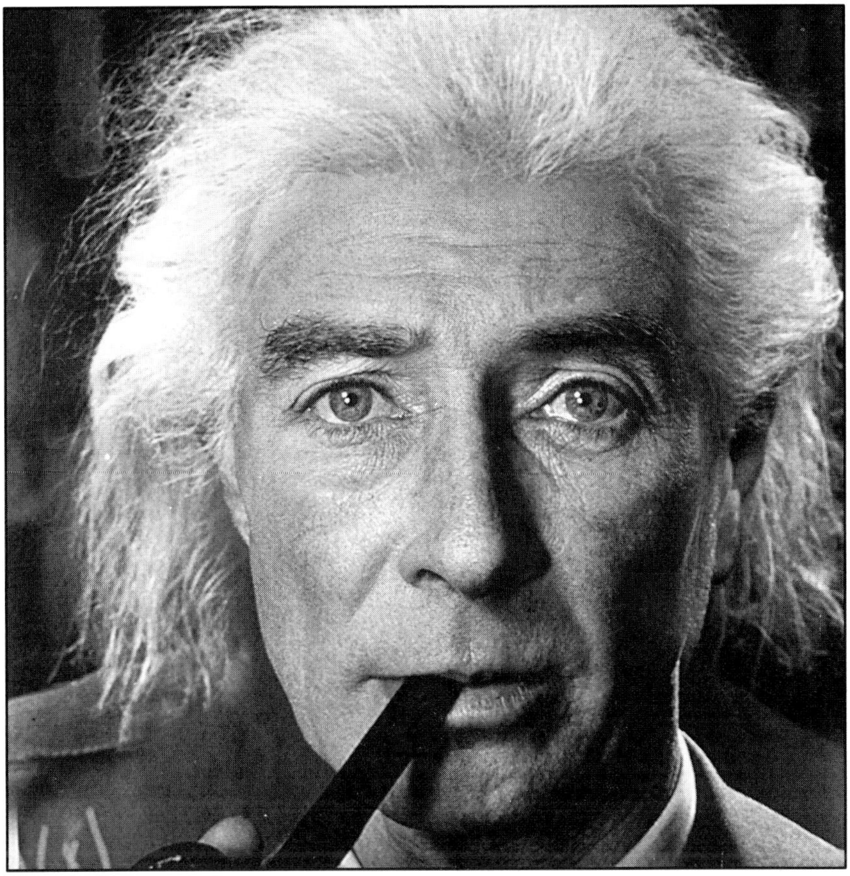

Opstein

4

Many transformations shown here result from merely wondering "what would happen if" some strange operation is applied to an image. In this case I wondered what would happen if all the dots in the picture were shifted down by an distance that varies with their brightness. In the picture language, this is written as

```
new[x,y-jlb[x,y]/4] = jlb[x,y]
```

where this time we change the index of the destination image instead of the source. The brighter the dot, the more it moves, with a maximum shift of `Z/4`. The portrait that was subjected to this operation is Jon Bentley's. Jon is a popular author of textbooks on program efficiency.* Here is first the original portrait, scanned in from a 4×5 inch black-and-white Polaroid picture.

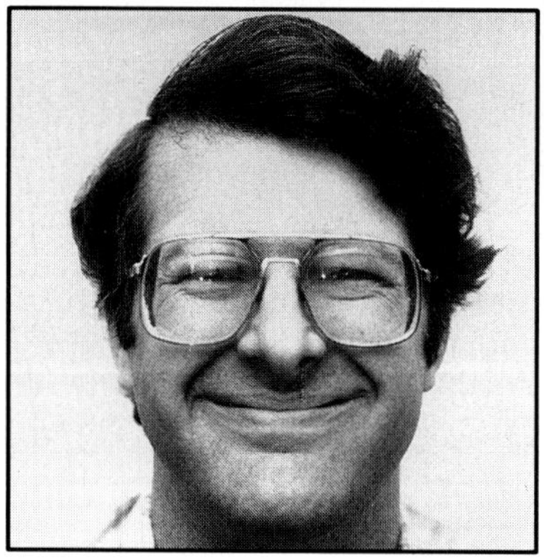

* Jon's best known books are *Writing Efficient Programs,* Prentice Hall, 1982, and *Programming Pearls,* Addison-Wesley, 1986.

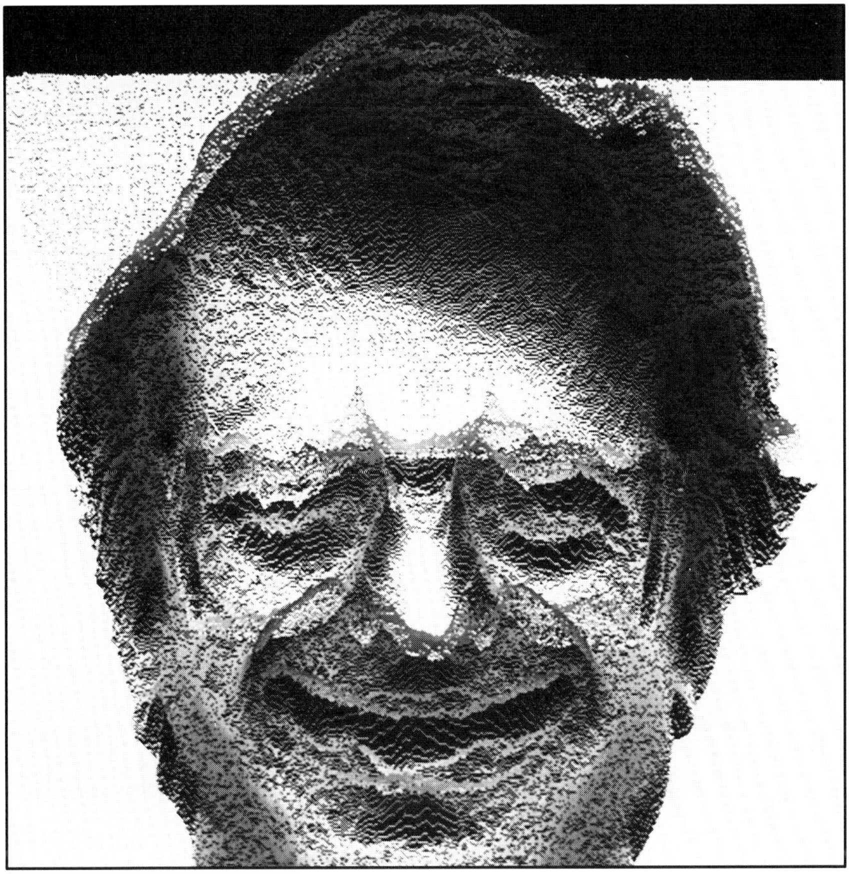

The Bentley Effect

5

For some reason, the portrait of Peter Weinberger has always been our most popular target for picture editing experiments. It started a few years ago when Peter was raised to the rank of department head and was careless enough to leave a portrait of himself floating around. On a goofy Saturday evening at the lab, Rob Pike and I started making photocopies and, to emphasize Peter's rise in the managerial hierarchy, prepared a chart of the Bell Labs Cabinet with his picture stuck in every available slot. Peter must have realized that the best he could do was not to react at all, if at least he wanted to avoid seeing his face 10 feet high on a water tower. Nevertheless, Peter's picture appeared and reappeared in the most unlikely places in the lab.

Within a few weeks after AT&T had revealed the new corporate logo, Tom Duff had made a Peter logo that has since become a symbol for our center. Rob Pike had T-shirts made. Ken Thompson ordered coffee mugs with the Peter logo. And, unavoidably, in the night of September 16, 1985, a Peter logo, 10 feet high, materialized on a water tower nearby. As an ill twist of fate, Peter has meanwhile become my department head at Bell Labs, which makes it very tempting to include him in this collection of faces. The picture was created by randomly selecting dots and sliding them down the page until a darker dot was met. The melting routine itself is included in Chapter **6**.

For comparison, an unedited version of Peter's face and the Peter logo are shown below.

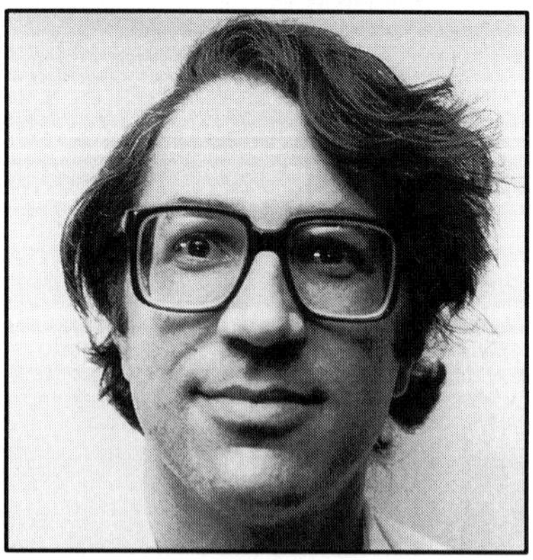

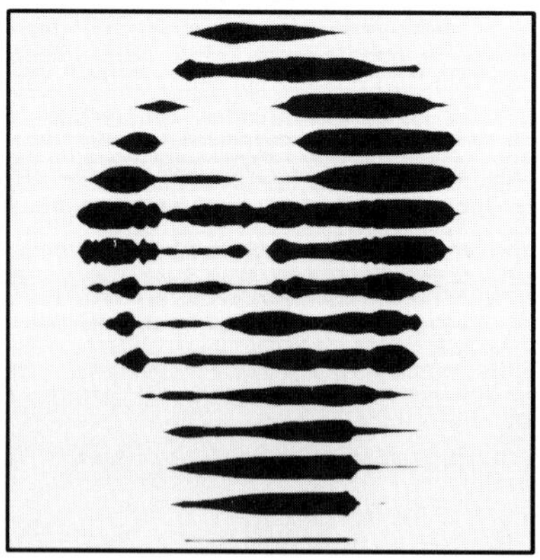

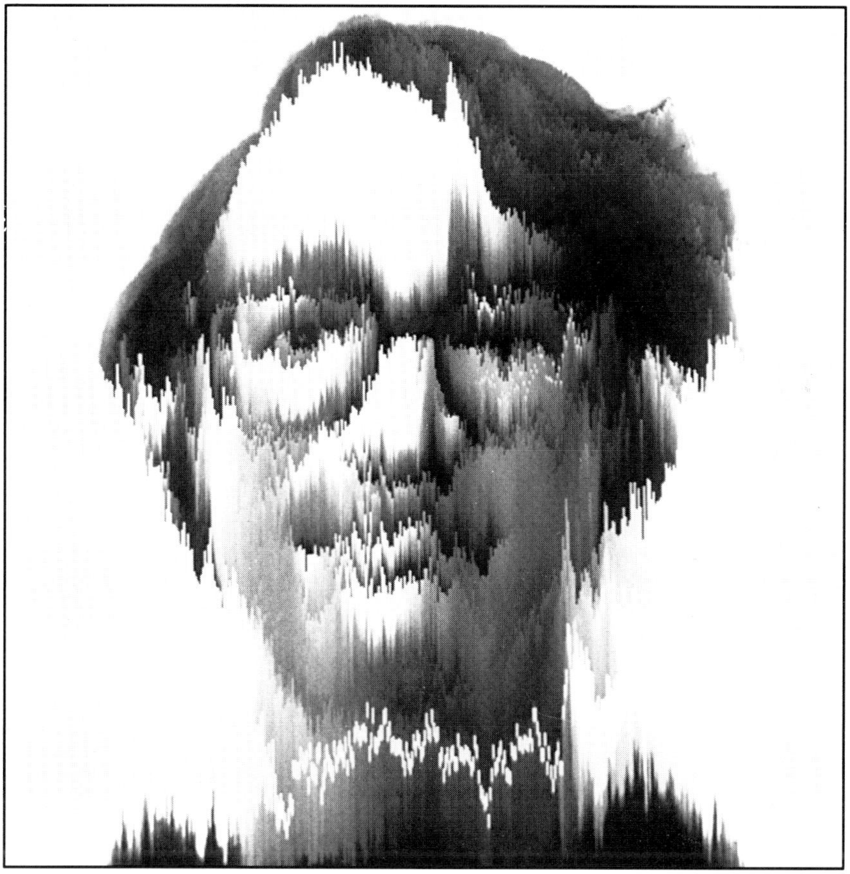

Peter Melted

6

With a few exceptions the more striking transformations seem to be the ones that are particularly easy to describe. On the title page for Chapter 3 we used a portrait twisted into a spiral. Here is the expression that makes it happen:

```
new[r,a] = ken[r, a+r/3]
```

The dots in the image are again addressed with polar coordinates. The angle `a` is incremented with a third of the radius `r`, thus making the edges swirl around the center of the picture.

The operation is applied to a portrait of Ken Thompson. Ken has left his mark at Bell Labs with the development, together with Dennis Ritchie, of the UNIX® operating system. Needless to say, the picture on the right does him no justice. His real unswirled portrait is shown below.

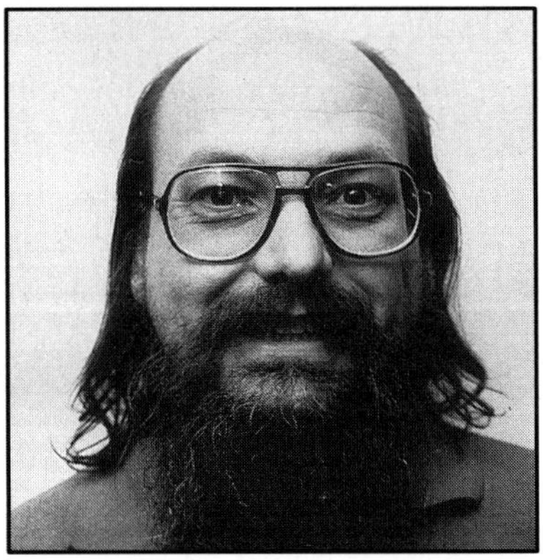

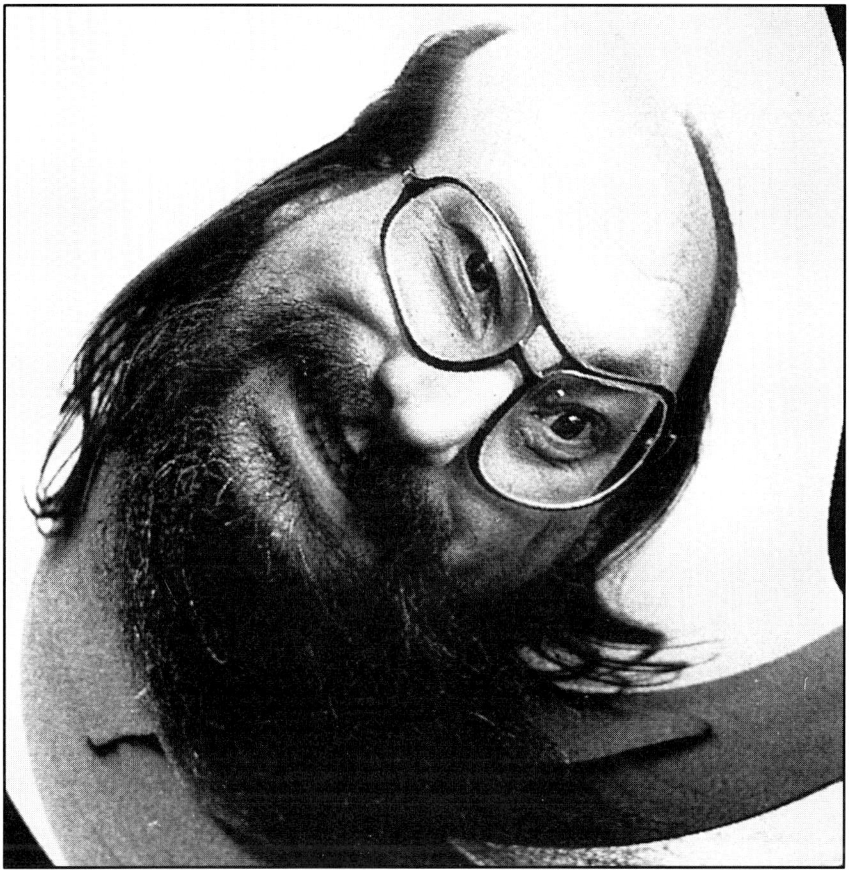

Ken Thompson

7

The painting-like effect of this transformation requires a little more work. For every dot in the image a program calculated a histogram of the surrounding 36 dots and assigned the value of the most frequently occurring brightness value. The result looks almost like an oil painting. In this case the portrait is of Dennis Ritchie. Dennis is of course best known for his work on UNIX and the *C* programming language. Locally, though, he is equally famous for his most impressive Halloween costumes. No picture transformation can achieve a comparable effect, so I won't even try: here is Dennis in oil. The transformation routine is included in Chapter **6**.

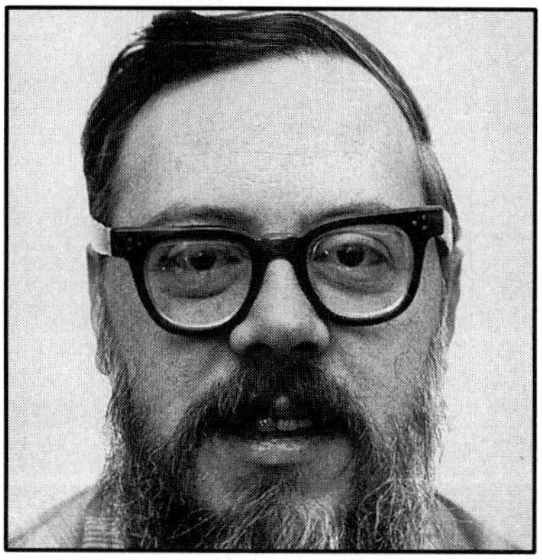

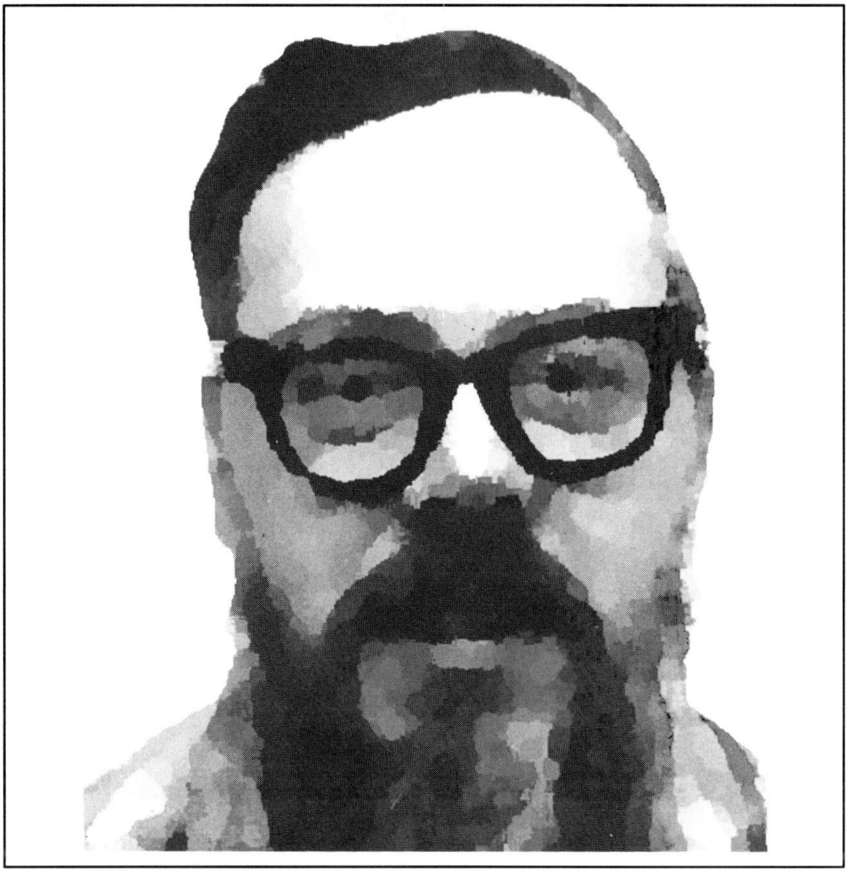

Dennis Ritchie

8

What if we took the polar coordinates of a dot and pretended they were Cartesian coordinates. That is, we use the angle `a` to calculate a value for the `x`-coordinate and the radius `r` to calculate the `y`. Let's say that we have a function `x(a)` to cast the `a` into an `x` and `y(r)` to cast the `r` into `y`. Adding scaling we can try the following expression:

```
new[x,y] = luca[x(a)*X/A, y(r)*Y/R]
```

The picture on the right is the result of this transformation applied to the portrait of Luca Cardelli, rotated by 90° to put him upright:

```
new[x,y] = old[Y-y, x]
```

It would be hard to maintain that computer graphics brings out the best in people. Below is a picture of the real Luca.

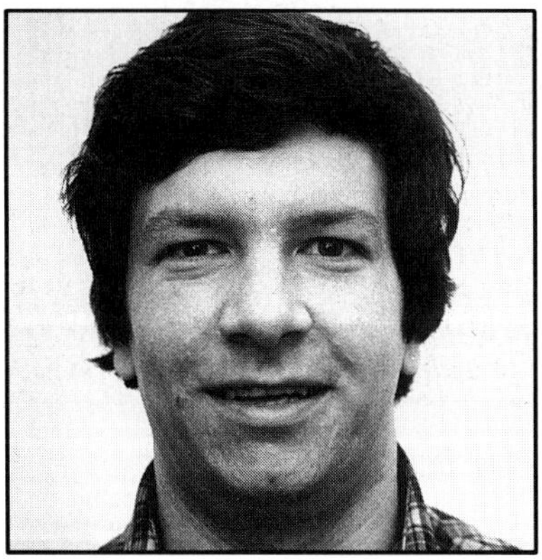

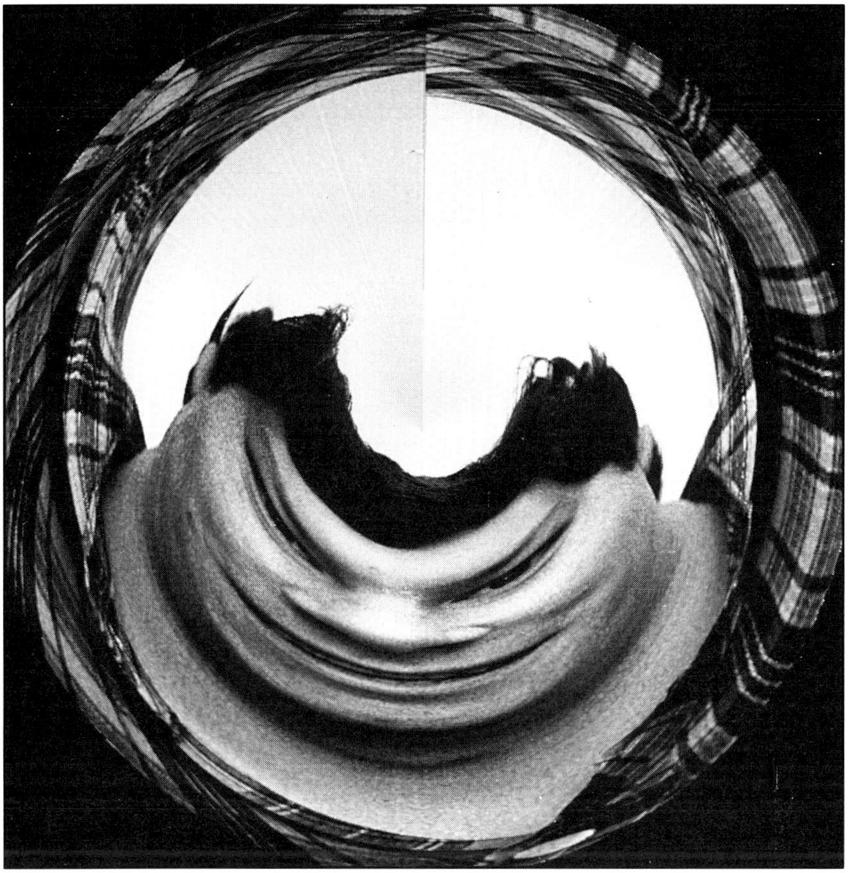

Luca Cardelli

9

The transformation shown here is similar to the one used for photo **2**. In this case a number of rows and columns are shifted at a time, with all numbers selected randomly. The amount of each shift was anywhere between 0 and 32 dots in either direction. The width of a shift was chosen randomly between 8 and 40 dots. See Chapter **6** for details.

The portrait used is that of Ed Sitar. Ed is a true magician with computer hardware and has achieved the impossible to keep machines running when they desperately want to be down. In fact, what you see on the right is probably what he feels on an average Monday when he is working on ten different major catastrophes at a time. But, in all fairness, below is a picture of what Ed really looks like.

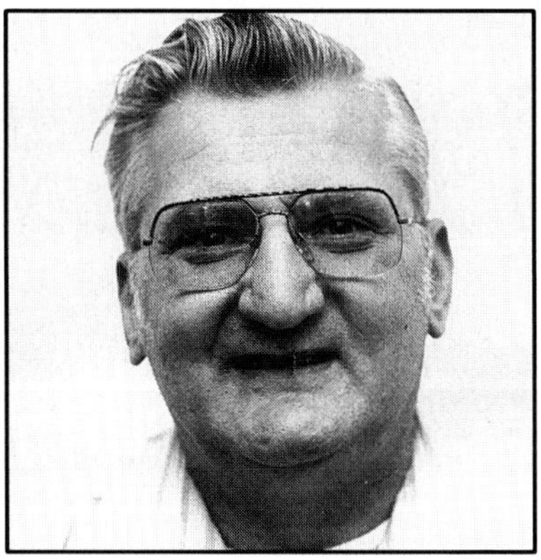

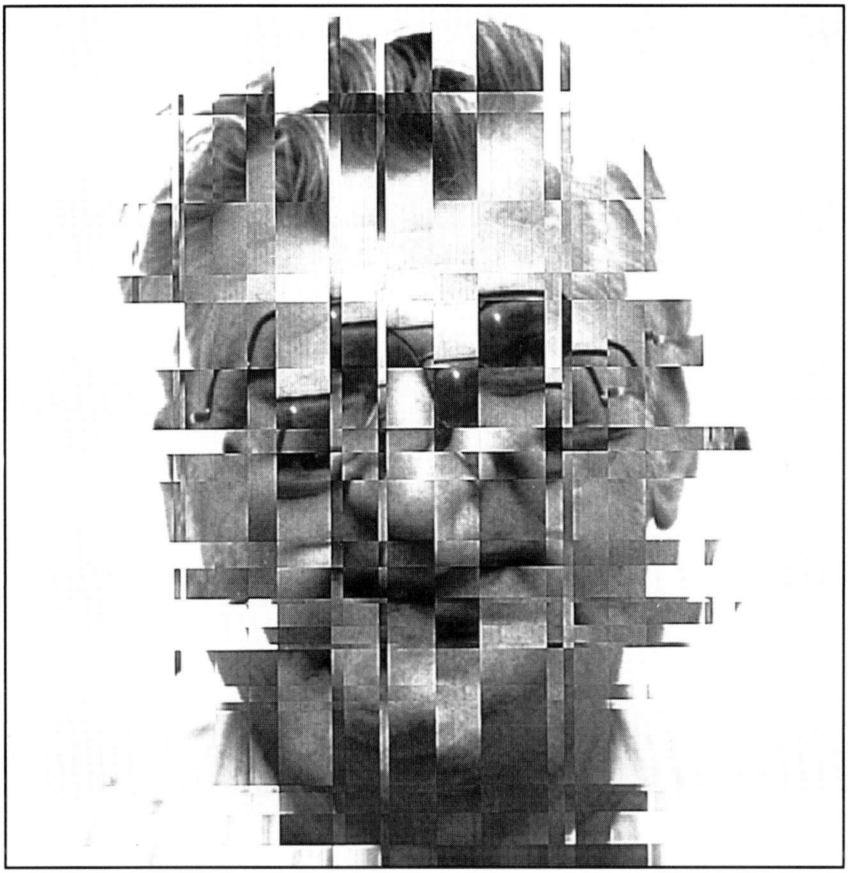

Ed Sitar

10

With a small library of photos of fairly standard patterns (e.g., wood grain, pebbles, brick, cloth) a range of new picture transformations becomes possible. Here we used a coarse picture of wood grain to transform a portrait of New York artist Hillary Burnett. The transformation is defined as follows:

```
new[x,y] = hillary[clamp(x-pattern*F),y]
```

where `F` is a factor that determines how large the distortion will be at each pixel. In the picture selected `F` was set to `3/4`, which means that each dot in the image was displaced up to `Z*3/4` columns depending on the brightness of the pattern. `clamp` is a function that protects against overflow or underflow of the calculated `x` index (it always returns a value between `0` and `X`).

The distorted picture was combined with the original, using an image matte to define the transition, as was done in photo 1. For comparison, here is also the original portrait and the pattern that was used.

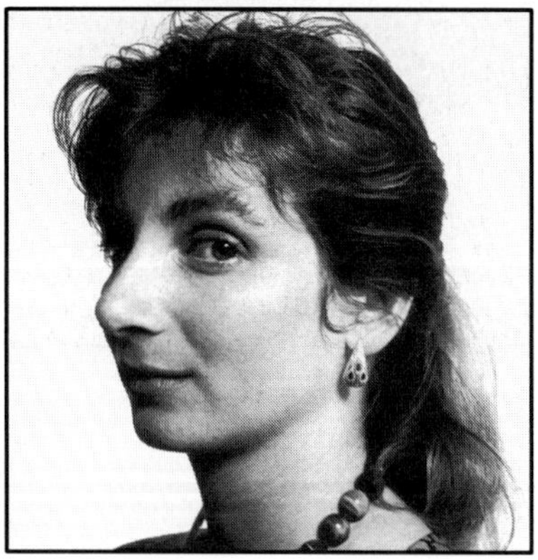

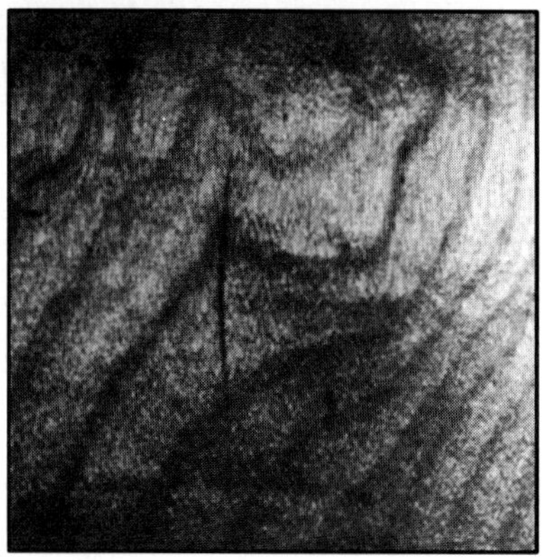

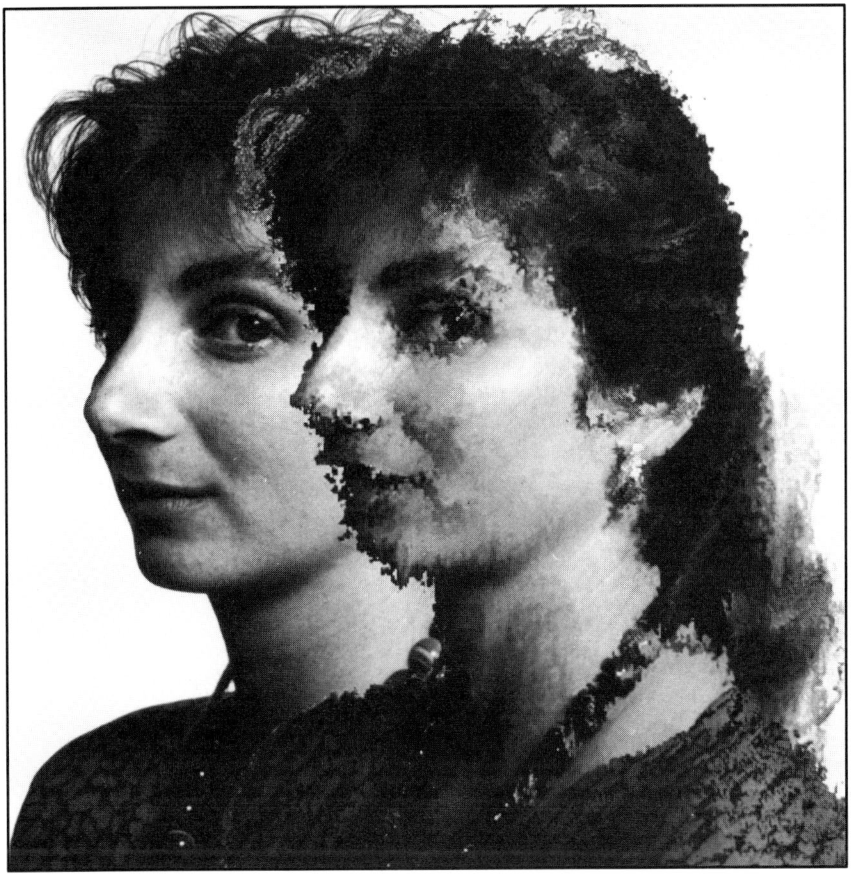

Warp

11

Here is a rather complex transformation expression that has a surprising op-art effect:

```
new[x,y] = greg[x,y]^(greg[x,y]*factor)>>17
```

where

```
factor = (128-(x-128)*(x-128) - (y-128)*(y-128))
```

A few operators in the expression will need some explanation. The circumflex operator used in the first expression is the exclusive or from the *C* programming language. The >> sign is a bitwise right shift of a value. In this case the shift by 17 positions is a fast way to get the effect of a division by 2^{17}.

Below is the original photo, a portrait of Greg Chesson. Greg is one of the contributors to the early versions of the UNIX operating system. As the transformation fittingly illustrates, Greg now lives in California.

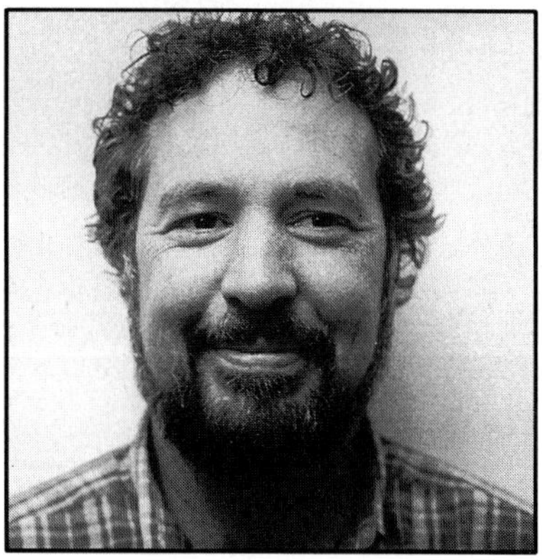

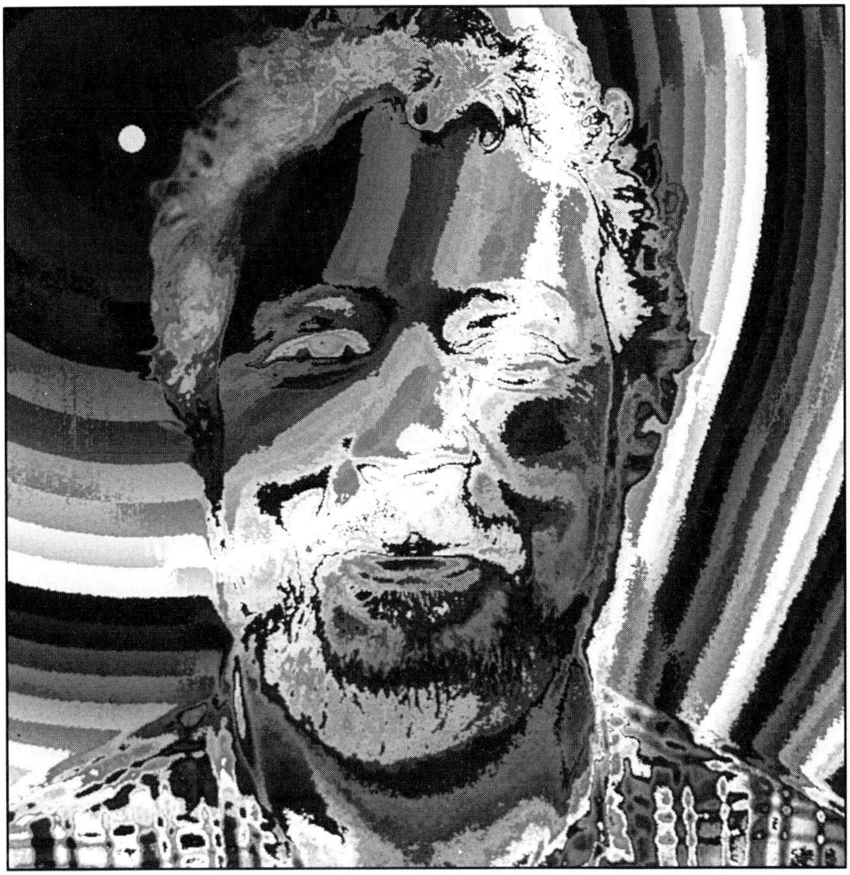

Gregory Chesson

12

The mirrors in a funhouse obviously work because the mirror surface is curved. The effect can be simulated with a simple `sine` function to index an image array. We have to experiment a little to find appropriate scaling factors, for instance to control the number of curves across the width of the image or the depth of each curve.

```
new[x,y] = ava[x+sin(C1*x)*C2,y+sin(y)*C3]
```

One appealing variant of this tranformation is shown below. The factors used for the picture on the right are `C1 = 1.15`, `C2 = 160`, and `C3 = 89`. The transformation is applied to the portrait of Al Aho. Every student in computer science is familiar with Al's books on algorithms and compiler design (known as the *dragon* books; see also the list of books at the end of Chapter 5). Here is a rare glimpse of the author in a funhouse mirror.

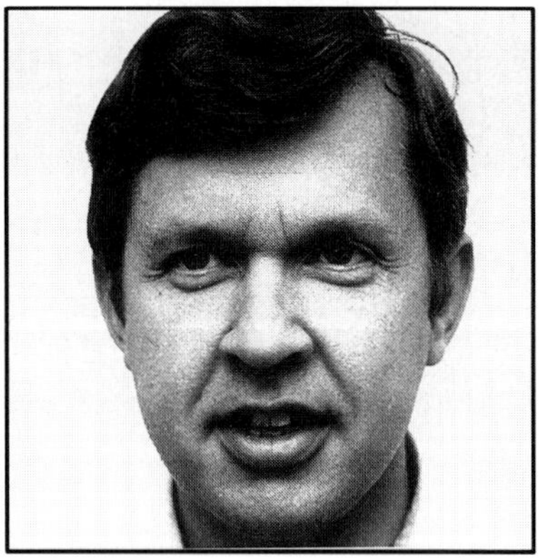

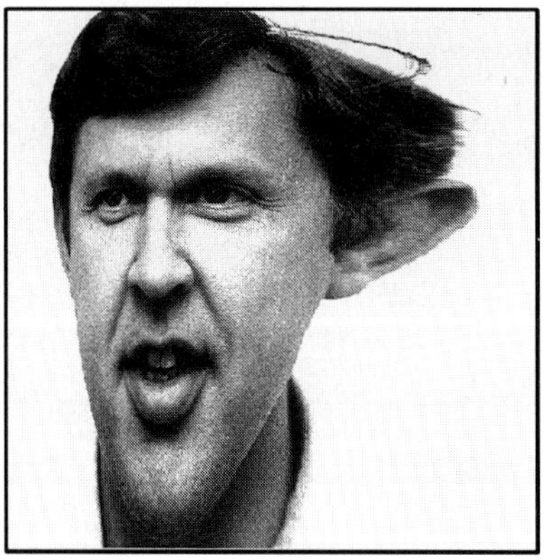

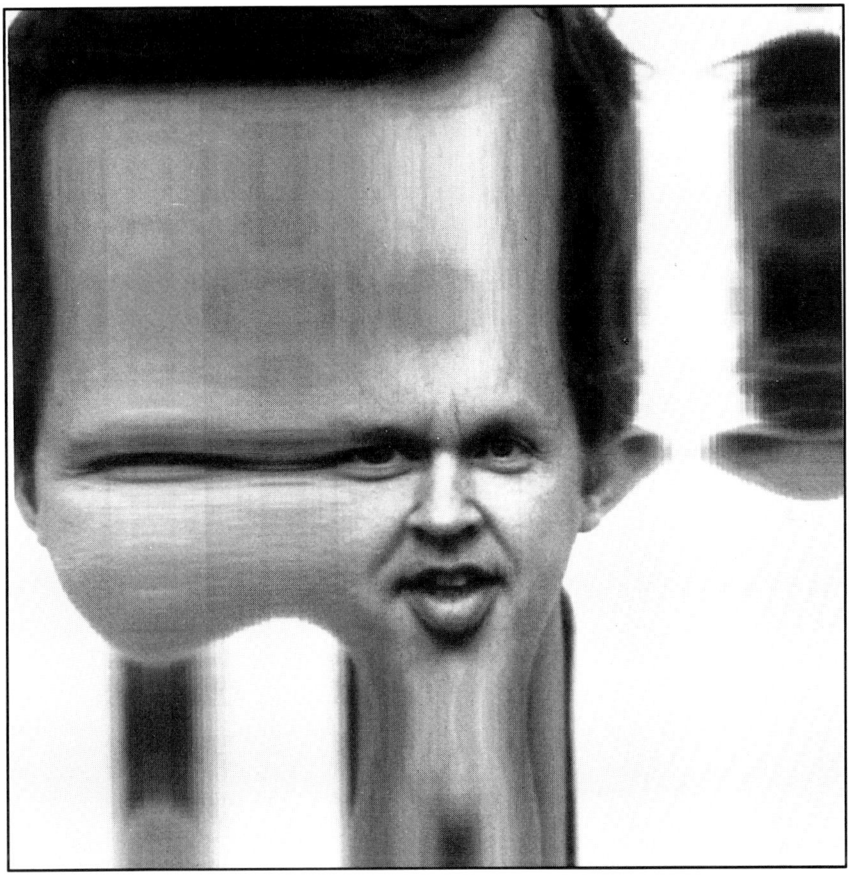

Al Aho

13

Well, if a funhouse mirror can be simulated with the computer, we should also be able to mimic the effect of looking through one of these wavy bathroom windows. This expression will do the trick:

```
new[x,y] = andrew[x+(x%32)-16,y]
```

Andrew Hume is a rugged Australian programmer, known throughout Bell Labs for a peculiar wardrobe that defies the seasons (shorts, even in the dead of winter).

The impact of transformation is enhanced somewhat if we add a spiraling effect, not seen in many bathroom windows.

```
new[x,y] = andrew[x+((a+r/10)%32)-16,y]
```

The result is shown on the right. Andrew's real portrait and the effect of the first transformation are shown below. And, yes, Andrew likes cats.

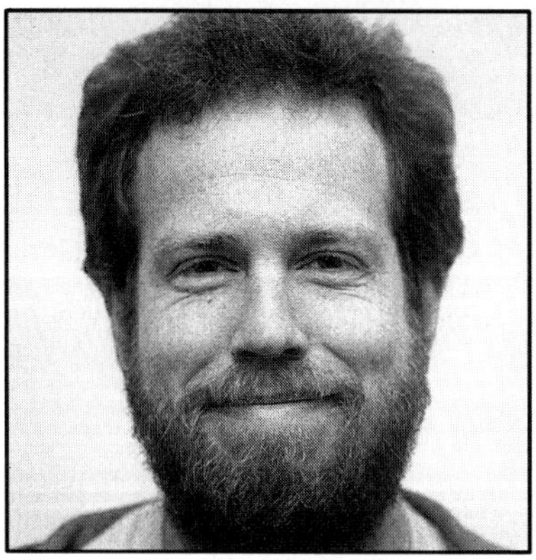

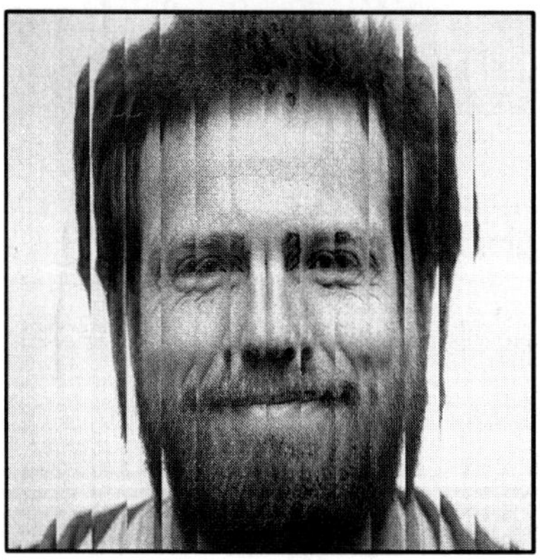

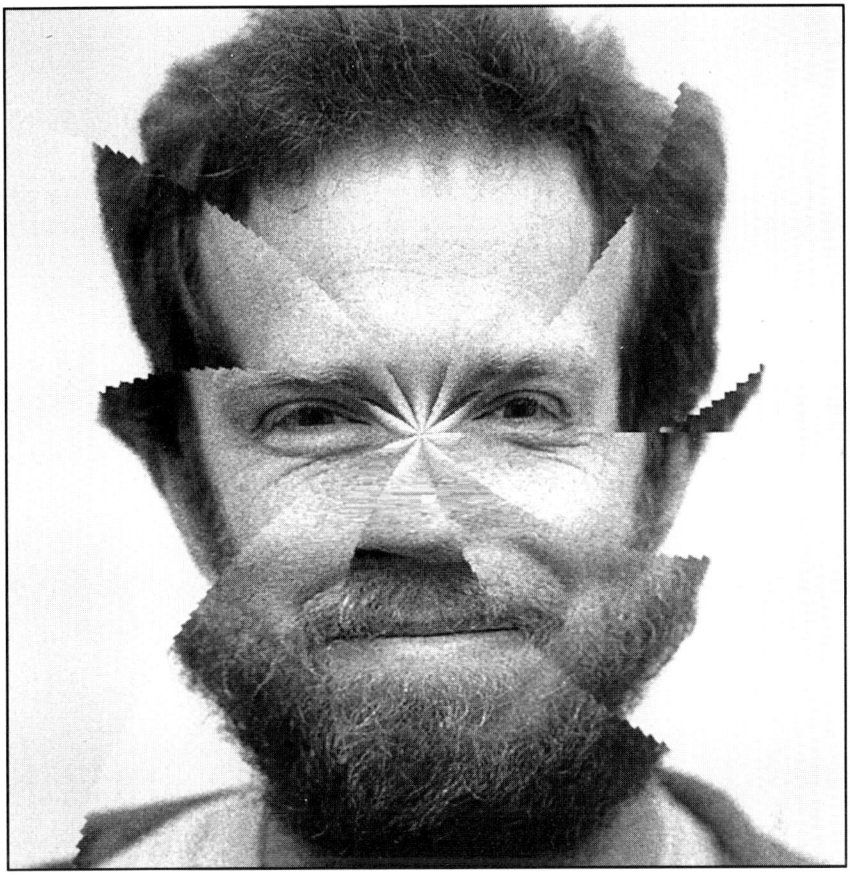

Andrew Humed

14

The obvious counterpart for the *caricature* transformation that was illustrated in the first of these images is the *fisheye*. Before our picture editor *pico* was even born, Tom Duff wrote a program that would simulate the effect of a fisheye lens. The effect can be mimicked with the following transformation, using polar coordinates:

```
new[r,a] = ps1[(r*r)/R,a]
```

The subject of this operation is Peter Langston. Peter worked at Lucasfilm for a while and is now with Bellcore. He is the author of popular computer games such as *empire* and *ballblazer*. The picture on which the transformation is based is shown below. In this case it is rather hard to decide which picture is more intriguing.

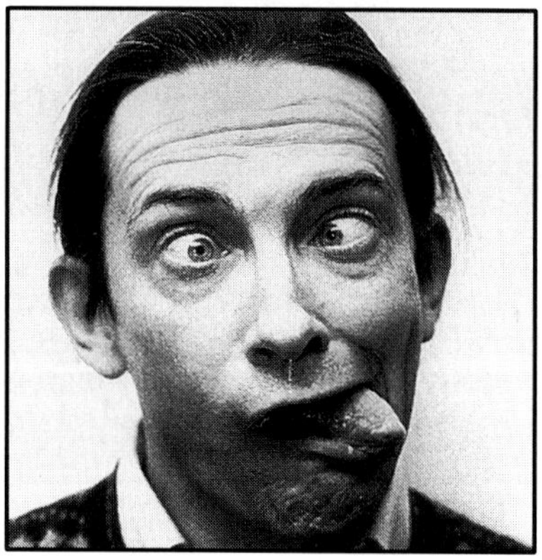

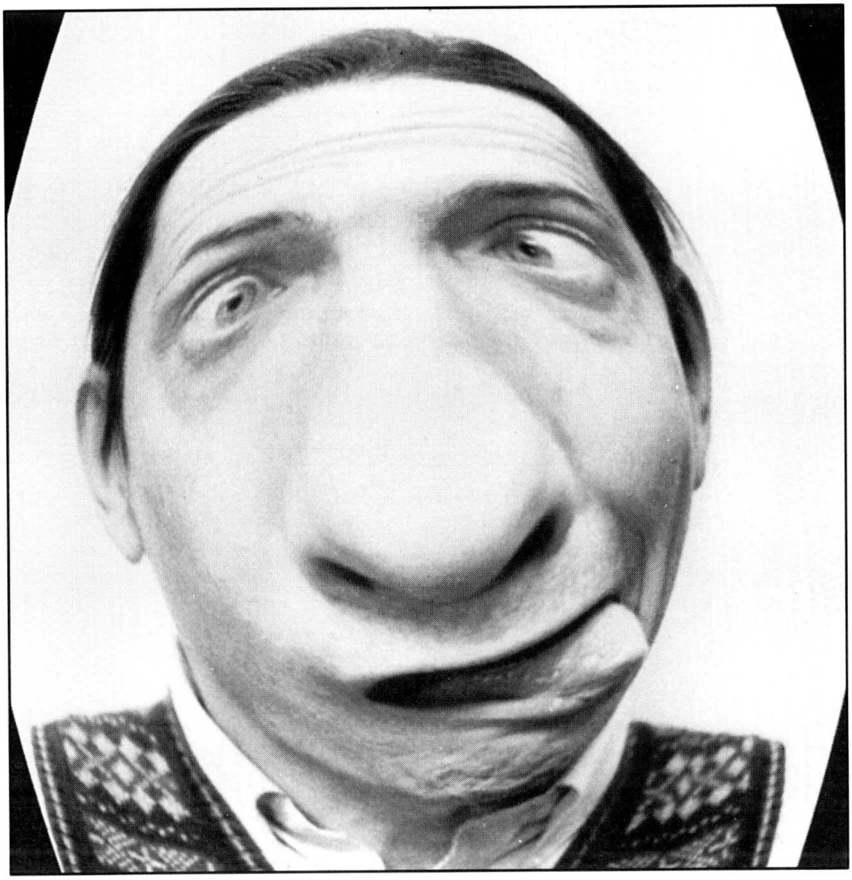

Fisheye

15

This is an example of a slightly more intricate transformation. The picture is sliced up into small squares which are moved by a random amount in the x and y direction. The background for the picture on the right is a negative of the original portrait (`new[x,y] = Z-theo[x,y]`). The tiling effect was obtained with a 10-line program written in the *pico* language. (A similar routine written in *C* is given in Chapter 6.) The portrait is of Theo Pavlidis, known for more serious contributions to the field of image analysis and image processing.*

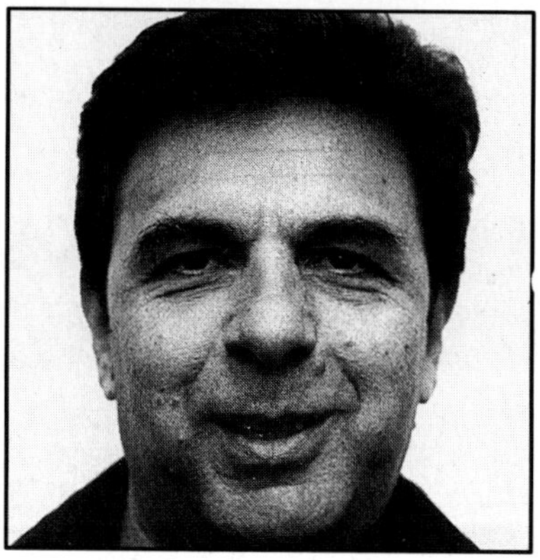

* For instance, *Algorithms for Graphics and Image Processing,* Computer Science Press, 1982.

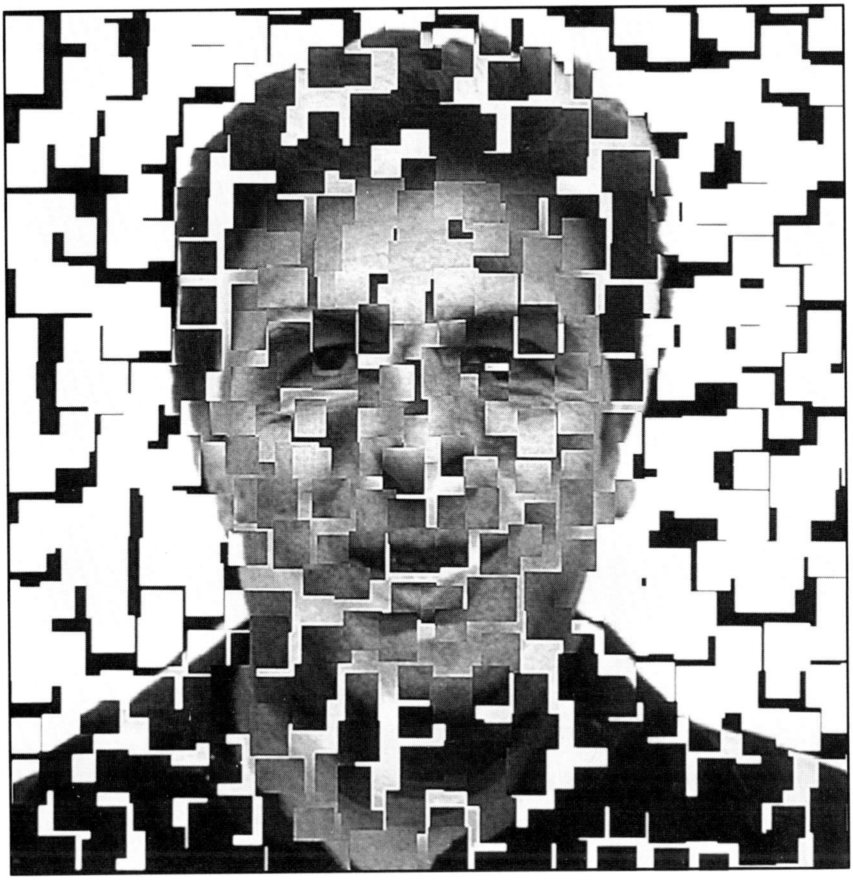

Tiled Theo

16

This is an example of the type of transformation that can be done with a *rubber-sheet* program. With such a program you can scale, stretch, and move parts of an image interactively. In this case it allows one to make either nasty or friendly variants of a neutral portrait such as Rob Pike's. Below the original and a friendlyfied variant; to the right a meaner version.

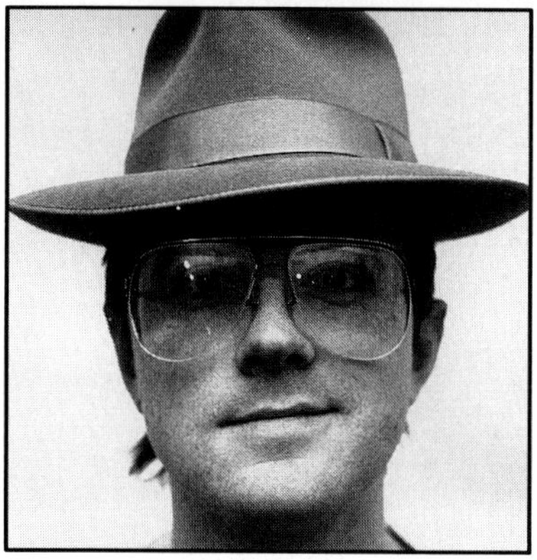

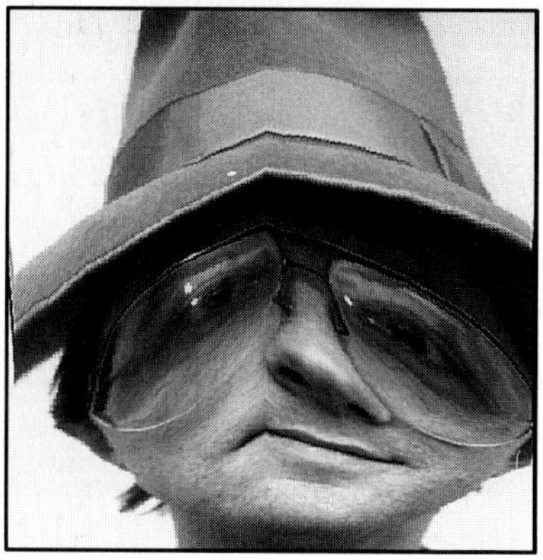

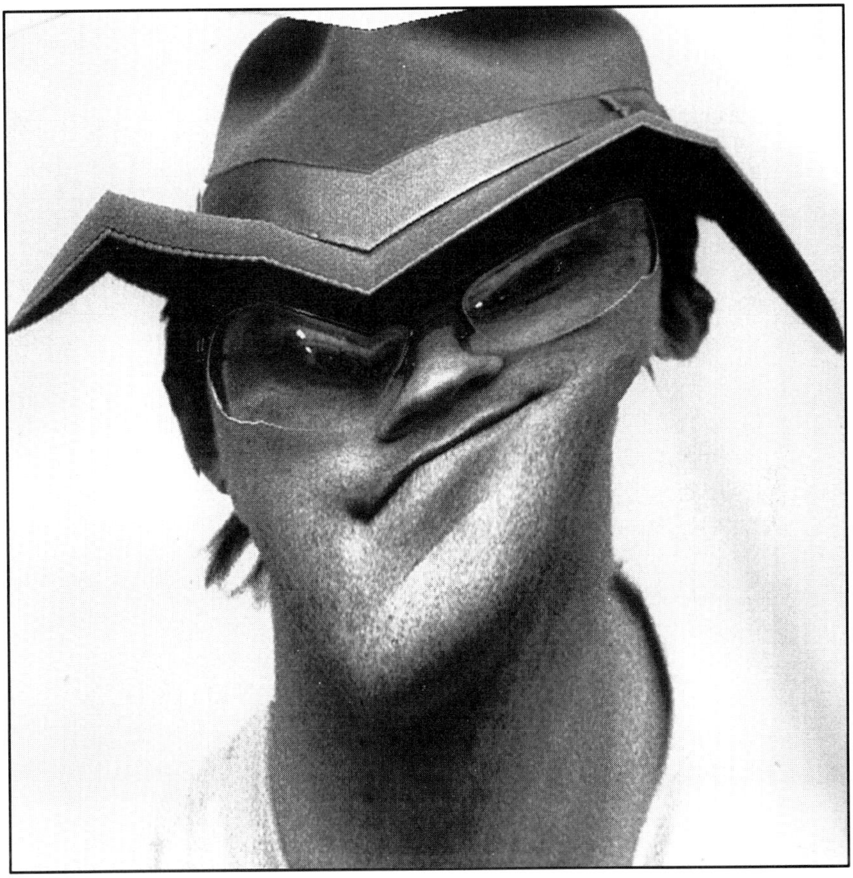

Mean Rob

17

After 16 "ordinary" transformations we can no longer avoid showing that, yes truly, a plastic surgeon could do wonders with software like this. When I first started exploring the possibilities of image transformations I wrote a little demonstration program, called "Pinocchio," that made the obvious change to a profile. At the time we had only two pictures in our data base with a profile: Bart Locanthi and Doug McIlroy. Since Doug McIlroy was my department head at the time, I courageously ran the program on his portrait. Sixteen frames from a little movie generated with the Pinocchio program are reproduced on the right. To my relief Doug does not hold it against me, and his children derive great joy from these pictures.

In the pictures on the right the nose was stretched. For comparison, in the small picture on the right below, the nose was shrunk. The original portrait is shown on the left. The Pinocchio images are mirrored.

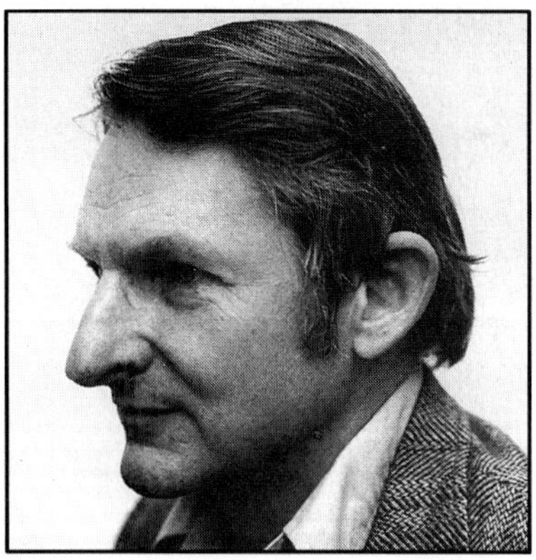

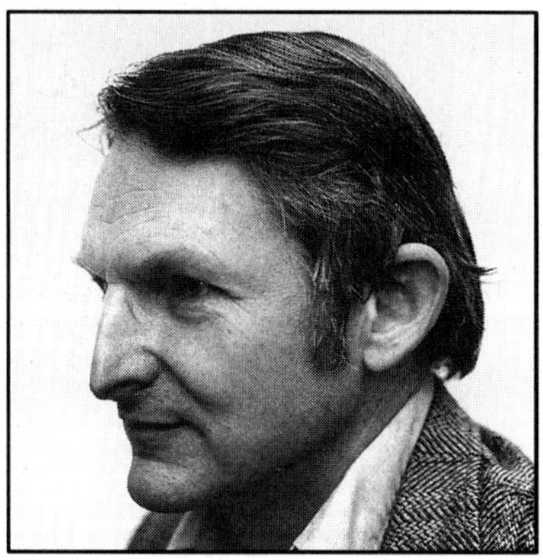

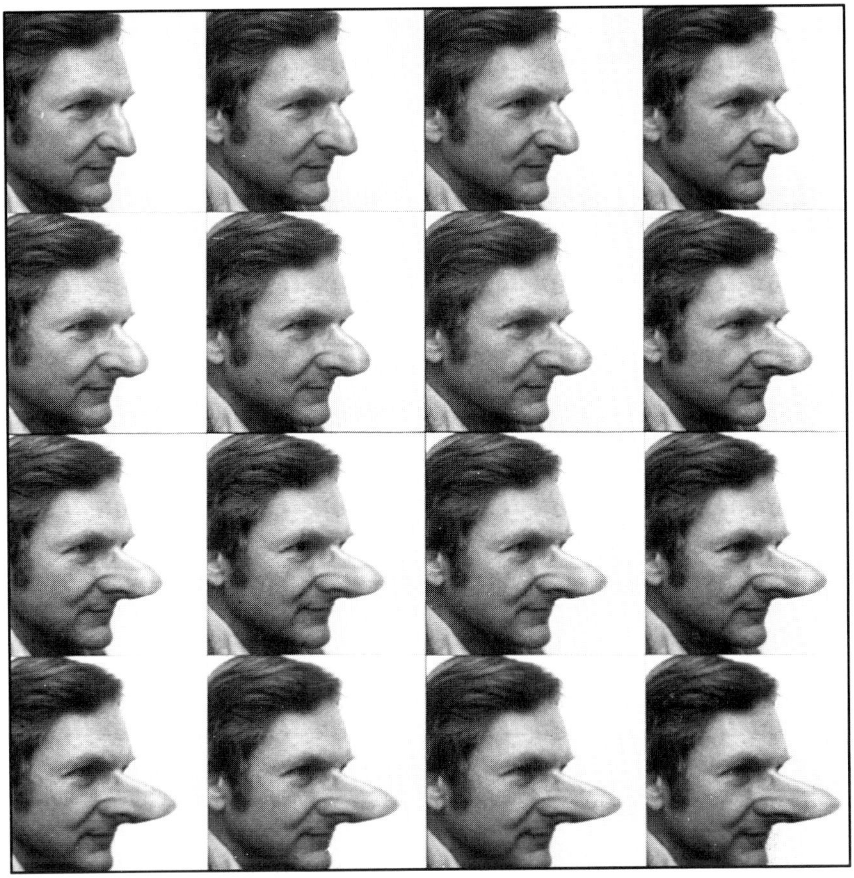

Pinocchio

18

The portrait that was used for this transformation has been a more or less standard test picture in digital image processing for almost 20 years. Everybody in image processing knows the image as the *Karen* picture. Yet nobody seems to know who Karen really is. Let history record that Karen's real name is Karen Nelson. Karen was a secretary at Bell Labs in the late sixties. She left the Labs in 1969, was married, and had four children. The Karen picture was first published in the *Bell System Technical Journal* of May/June 1969.

In the picture on the right a combination of a few earlier transformations is used. This is the expression:

```
new[r,a] = karen[r, a + karen[r,a]/8]
```

The angle `a` is incremented with an amount that depends on the brightness of the image at that spot. The result is much like a spin-painting.

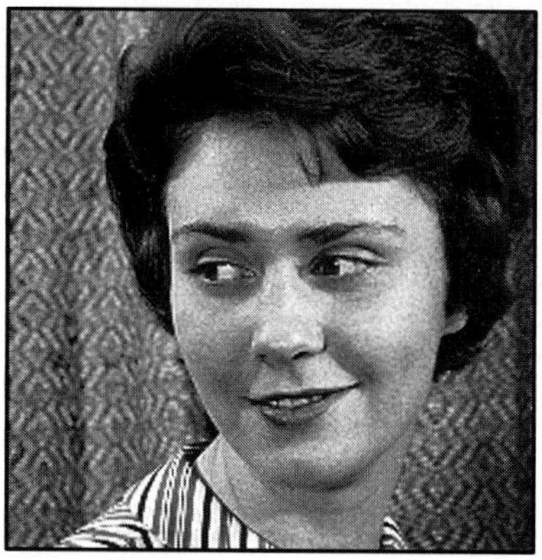

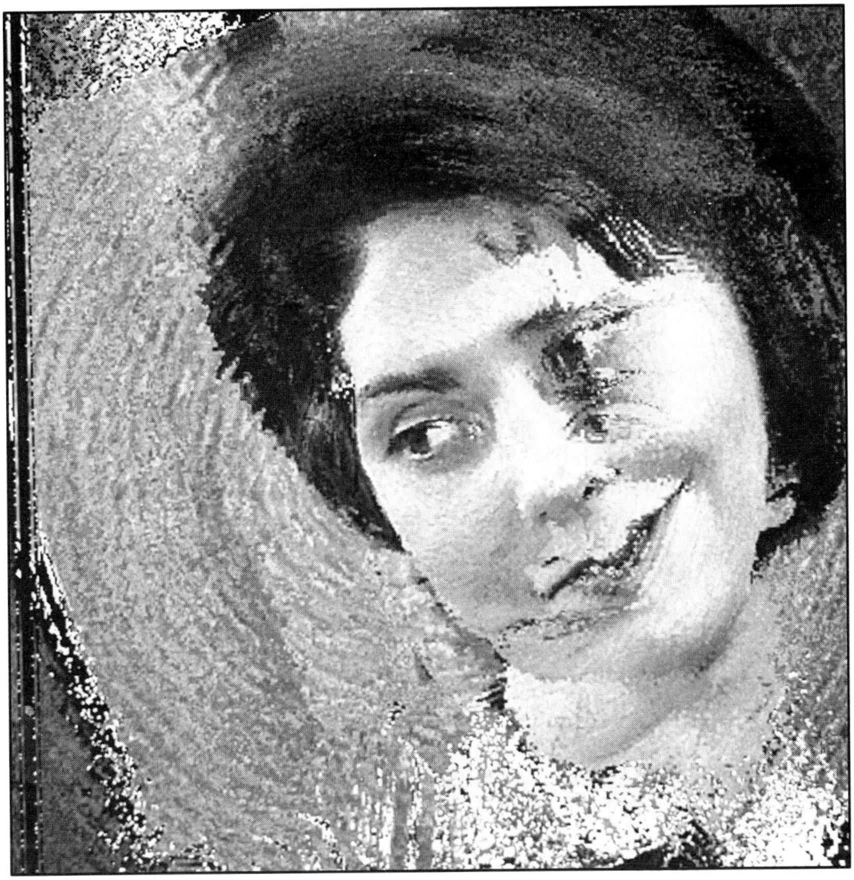

Karen

19

Perhaps one picture in this series is in order to illustrate that one can, of course, use the digital darkroom tools to just plainly enhance a photo without distorting it. The picture on the right is a composite of two photos and an artificial background. The original portrait is shown below. To reduce the highlight on the hair and to replace the background I made two separate image mattes (see Chapter 6). The mattes are blurred to smooth the edges. The background is generated with the expression

```
new[x,y] = (x/2)(y/2)
```

The composite of foreground image `F` and background image `B` using `matte` (shown below) is accomplished with the following image arithmetic:

```
new[x,y] = ((matte[x,y]*F[x,y]+(Z-matte[x,y])*B[x,y])/Z
```

We can use smaller mattes in the same manner to darken highlights (called "burning in" in conventional photography). The portrait is of Lillian Schwartz, a seasoned pro in the art of computer graphics.

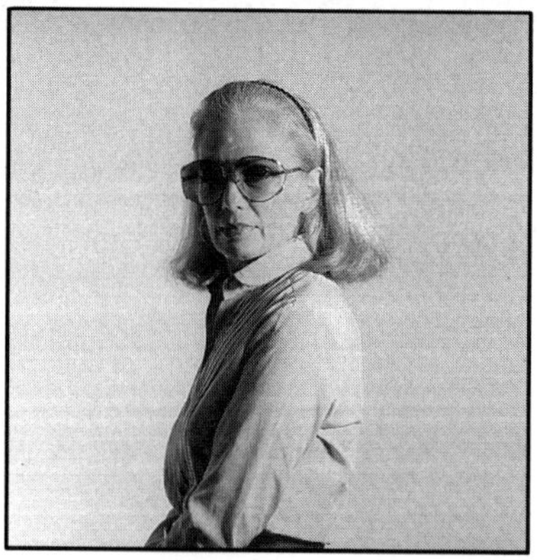

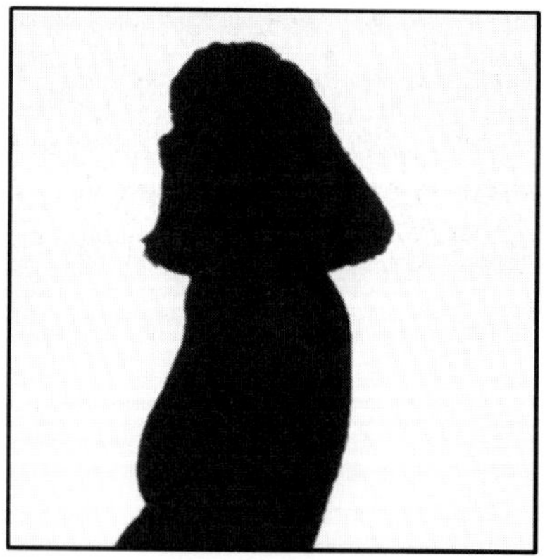

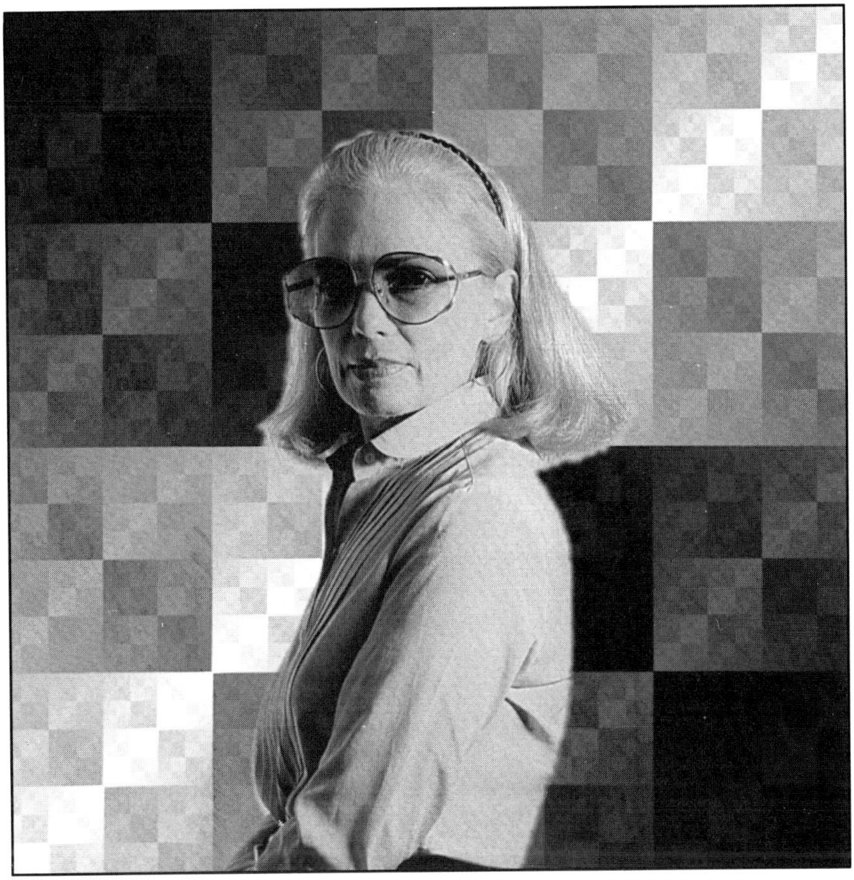

Lillian Schwartz

20

Many years ago, Leon D. Harmon of Bell Labs studied the recognizability of faces, depending on the resolution at which they were reproduced.* One image from his series made history: a low resolution, but perfectly recognizable, image of president Lincoln. The transformation is quite simple to mimic in the picture language.

```
new[x,y] = old[(x/16)*16,(y/16)*16]
```

We use a truncation here that is implicit in integer arithmetic. Note that 156/16 = 9.75 which, when stored as an integer, truncates to 9. Therefore (156/16) * 16 = 144 and not 156.

The result of the transformation is shown below, together with the original portrait of Judy Paone, secretary in our Computing Techniques Research department. Since recognizability is not really an issue in this book, we can do even better, for instance, by switching to polar coordinates

```
new[r,a] = old[(r/32)*32,(a/32)*32]
```

The result of this transformation is shown on the right.

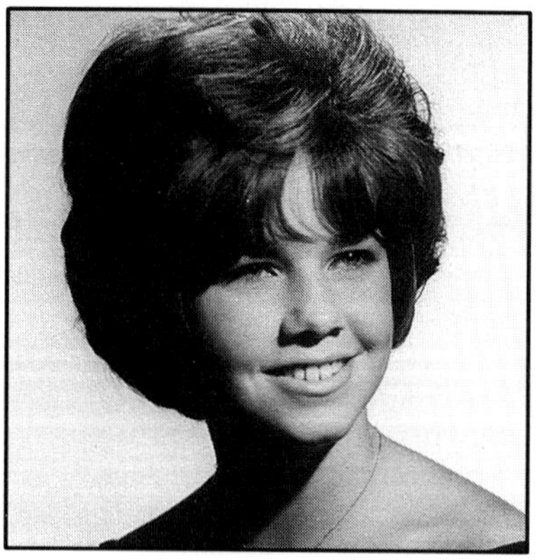

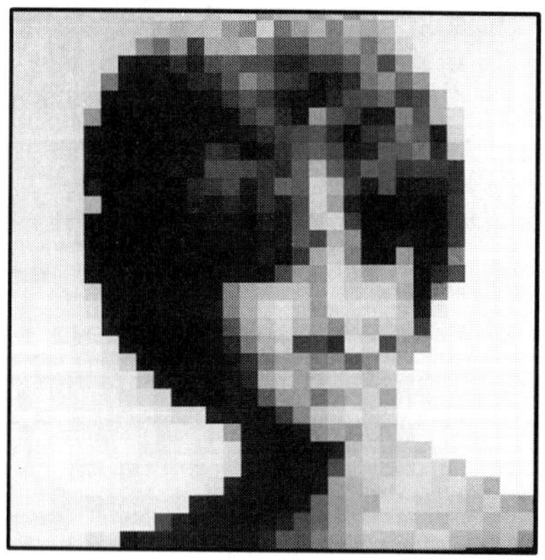

---

* See, for instance, his article "The recognition of faces," in *Scientific Amercican*, November 1973, p. 71.

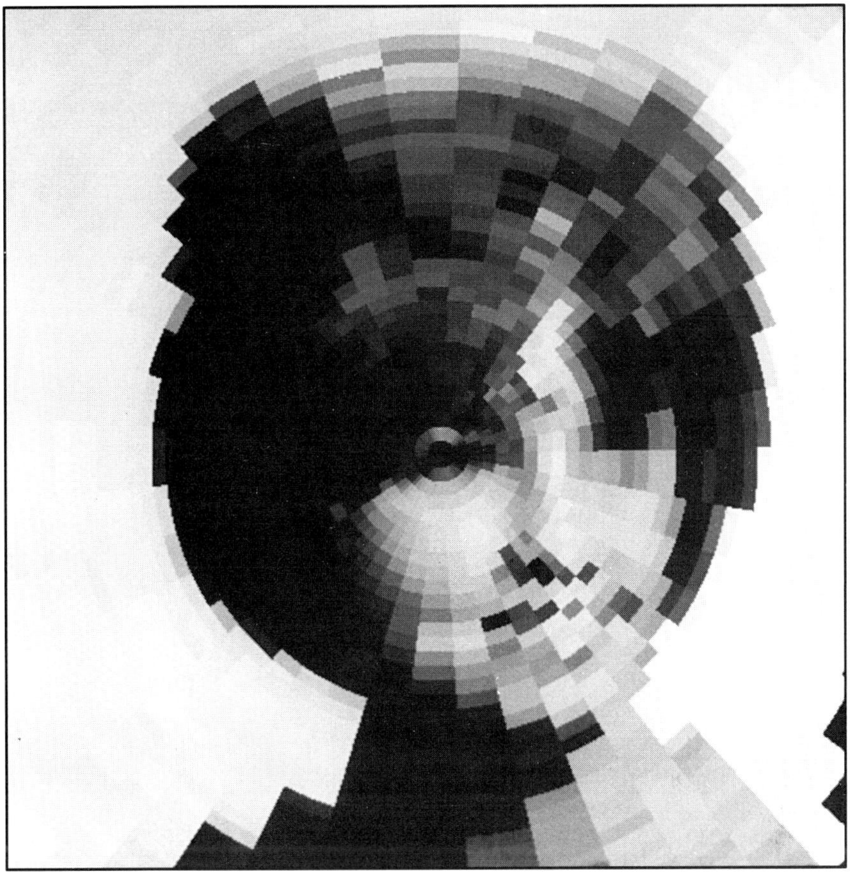

The Lincoln Transform

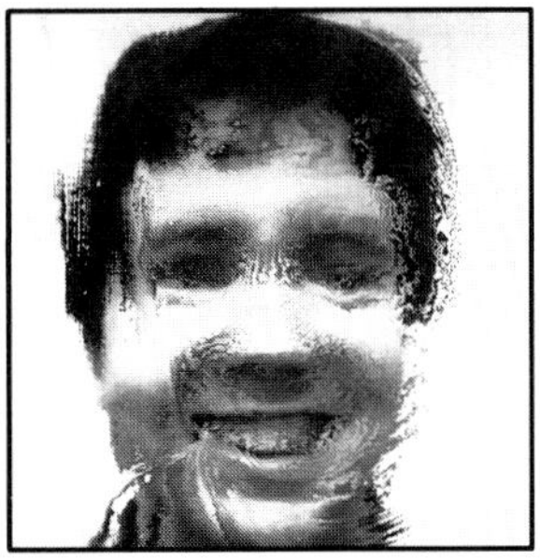

5 Darkroom Software

If you have a home computer, some way to display a graphics image, and maybe even a way to capture images from a digitizer or a video recorder, you can easily build your own digital darkroom tools. To help you get started I will discuss a small interactive image editor named *popi* (pronounced "po-pee"). It is a portable version of the editor *pico* ("pee-ko") that was used to generate the pictures in this book. (*Popi* is short for *portable pico.*)

The most noticeable difference between *pico* and *popi* is speed. *Pico* has a built-in optimizing compiler that translates transformation expressions into machine code for a DEC VAX computer. This compiler dramatically improves the performance of the editor, but of course, it works for only one specific target machine. Instead, *popi* translates the transformation expressions into programs that are interpreted by a little portable stack machine. This reduces the efficiency, but makes it possible to use the editor on any machine that can compile *C* programs.

Popi

The discussion that follows explains how *popi* works, how you can use it to create and edit images, and how user commands are parsed and executed. The editor is for black-and-white images, stored in disk files in raw format: one byte per pixel in scanline order, top scanline first. There are a few other restrictions to *popi*'s command language that you may or may not want to remove once you have this software running on your system. This version of the editor, for instance, does not know any trigonometric functions and does not know about polar coordinates. It will be relatively easy to make the extensions. Some hints on how to do that are given at the end of this chapter.

The resolution of the images you can process depends only on the amount of memory available on your system. The more memory, the better. The version discussed here works with 248×248 images, for which you will at least need 200 kilobytes of main memory in your system.

Command Language

Popi accepts five types of commands. The most important one is the image transformation command

```
new = expression
```

that was used throughout this book. The other commands are

```
r file
```

to read an image from a disk file into a read-only buffer,

```
w file
```

to write the result of the last transformation into a file,

```
f
```

to show which files are currently open, and

```
q
```

to quit the editor.

Let us ignore the precise structure of the transformation expressions for a while. We return to that in the section titled *Grammar Rules*. We look first at the global structure of the editor. Commands can be typed on a single line separated by semicolons, or on separate lines. An edit session with *popi*, for instance, may go as follows.

```
$ popi
-> r rob            read image 'rob' into a buffer
-> r pjw            read image 'pjw' into a buffer
-> f                check which files are open
$1 = rob
$2 = pjw
-> new=rob-pjw      subtract pjw from rob
-> w prob           write result in a file 'prob'
-> q                quit
$                   operating system prompt
```

The arrow `->` is the editor's prompt: it tells the user that the program is ready for a new command.

Program Structure

The image editor is written in the programming language *C*. It has four parts:

- a lexical analyzer,
- a recursive-descent parser,
- a file handler, and
- an interpreter, built as a stack-machine.

The figure illustrates how these parts fit together.

Consider what happens when the user (at the upper left-hand side of the figure) enters the command **new=x**y**. The command is first read by the lexical analyzer. The job of the lexical analyzer is to recognize some predefined character sequences in the input, such as the image name **new** and the operator ******. Each predefined sequence is passed as a single *token* to the next program module: the parser. The eight-character sequence **new=x**y** is passed as a sequence of five tokens (**new**, **=**, **x**, **POW**, and **y**) from the lexical analyzer to the parser.

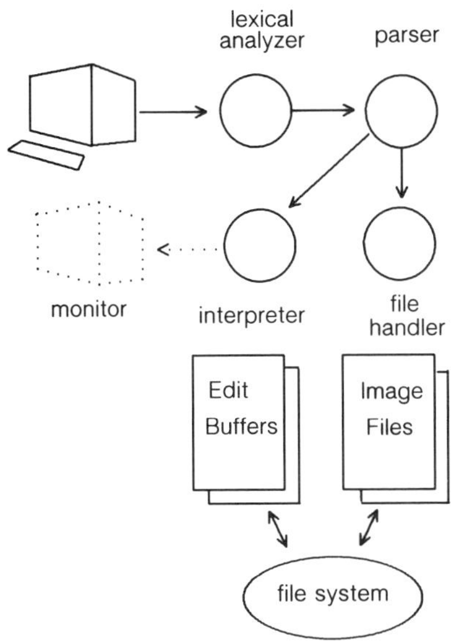

The Structure of Popi

The parser looks at the sequence of tokens and decides what type of command it is. In this case it will decide that this is an image transformation command since the first token is **new** and not, for example, **r** or **w**. The parser then starts building a little program for the interpreter to perform the transformation. For our example the program should instruct the interpreter to calculate a new value x^y for each pixel (dot) of the image. The execution loop over all pixels is a fixed part of the interpreter. Note that the interpreter evaluates the complete transformation expression once for every pixel in the image being edited.

If the user types the command **r picture**, the parser will invoke the file handler to read the image stored in file **picture**. The image is read into a read-only buffer and can be used as a source for image edit operations. The only images that ever change during an edit session are the ones in the edit buffers. There are two edit buffers: one is called **new** and the other is called **old**. Buffer **old** holds the result of the last edit operation performed. Initially it is an all-zero, or black, image. The other edit buffer, **new**, is the target of the current edit operation. After the completion of each edit operation the two buffers are swapped; the result of the last edit operation becomes the start for a next one. (Note that this makes it trivial to add a one-level *undo* operation.)

You will almost certainly want to extend the editor with a display routine, dotted in the figure, to see the transformations on a monitor either while they are being performed by the interpreter, or after the interpreter completes. The specific display routine you will need, however, depends on the hardware you use. A sample routine for bi-level displays is included at the end of this chapter.

Throughout the program, library routines are used that can in one form or another be found on most systems. All library routines used are part of the proposed *ANSI* standard *C* language definition, so it should be fairly easy to find or to provide for equivalent routines on most systems. The software should run without change on well-known systems such as UNIX and MS-DOS.

Let's take a closer look now at the different parts of the editor. At the end of this chapter the complete program is listed.

The Lexical Analyzer

The task of the lexical analyzer is to recognize keywords such as **`new`** and `old`, and identify operators that consist of more than one character, such as `>=`, `!=`, and `&&`. It must also find out when the name of an image file is used, and it must recognize numbers and convert the corresponding character strings into integers. White space (space and tab characters) is ignored. Everything that is not recognized by the lexical analyzer is passed on to the parser untouched. Single characters which are not part of a predefined sequence are treated as tokens with a code that equals their ASCII value. All other tokens are written in capitals, e.g., **`POW`**, and are defined as integer constants with a value greater than 255, the largest possible ASCII value.

The function `getchar()` is a library routine that returns the next available character in the command typed by the user.

The tokens passed from the lexical analyzer to the parser can have two attributes: `lexval` and `text`. They are declared as follows.

```
int lexval;
char text[256];
```

Tokens of the type **`VALUE`**, for example, have a value attribute stored in the integer variable `lexval`. Tokens of type **`NAME`** have a string attribute that is stored in array `text`. Tokens of type **`FNAME`** have both a value and a string attribute. The **`FNAME`** token refers to an open image file. Its string attribute gives the file name, and its value attribute is the number of the buffer into which the image was read.

This is what the lexical analyzer looks like:

```
lex()
{       int c;

        do      /* ignore white space */
                c = getchar();
        while (c == ' ' || c == '\t');

        if (isdigit(c))
                c = getnumber(c);
        else if (isalpha(c) || c == '_')
                c = getstring(c);

        switch (c) {
        case EOF:  c = 'q'; break;
        case '*':  c = follow('*', POW, c); break;
        case '>':  c = follow('=', GE,  c); break;
        case '<':  c = follow('=', LE,  c); break;
        case '!':  c = follow('=', NE,  c); break;
        case '=':  c = follow('=', EQ,  c); break;
        case '|':  c = follow('|', OR,  c); break;
        case '&':  c = follow('&', AND, c); break;
        case 'Z':  c = VALUE; lexval = 255; break;
        case 'Y':  c = VALUE; lexval = DEF_Y-1; break;
        case 'X':  c = VALUE; lexval = DEF_X-1; break;
        default :  break;
        }
        return c;
}
```

The function `follow(tok,ifyes,ifno)` looks at the next character typed. If it matches `tok`, the value `ifyes` is returned; if it does not match, the character is saved with `pushback()` (more about that below) and `ifno` is returned.

```
follow(tok, ifyes, ifno)
{       int c;

        if ((c = getchar()) == tok)
                return ifyes;
        pushback(c);

        return ifno;
}
```

The library routines `isdigit(c)` and `isalpha(c)` return nonzero (a boolean value `true` in *C*) when the argument is a digit or a letter, respectively. `getnumber(c)` and `getstring(c)` are shown below. They scan the user command for a number or a text string starting with character `c`.

```
getnumber(first)
{       int c;

        lexval = first - '0';
        while (isdigit(c = getchar()))
                lexval = 10*lexval + c - '0';
        pushback(c);
        return VALUE;
}
```

File names are looked up in a structure `src[]` where the I/O handler stores images. `nsrc` slots are in use, but the first two slots (0 and 1) are for the edit buffers and are skipped in the search. We will talk more about this data structure in a little while.

```
getstring(first)
{       int c = first;
        char *str = text;

        do {
                *str++ = c;
                c = getchar();
        } while (isalpha(c) || c == '_' || isdigit(c));
        *str = '\0';
        pushback(c);

        if (strcmp(text, "new") == 0) return NEW;
        if (strcmp(text, "old") == 0) return OLD;

        for (c = 2; c < nsrc; c++)
                if (strcmp(src[c].str, text) == 0)
                {       lexval = c-1;
                        return FNAME;
                }
        if (strlen(text) > 1)
                return NAME;
        return first;
}
```

A few more library routines are used here. `strlen(str)` returns the number of characters in the string, and `strcmp(str1,str2)` returns zero if the two given strings are equal. Normally, the lines with the function calls to `strcmp()` would be implemented as a search in a symbol table, but since we have only a few predefined symbols in this program, we can easily do without.

The last character read by routines `follow()`, `getnumber()`, and `getstring()` terminates a symbol and may start the next one. It must be saved for later, so it is pushed back onto the input. The function `pushback(c)` can be implemented with a one-slot buffer. In a UNIX environment it can be implemented as `ungetc(c,stdin)`.

The Parser

Apart from correctly decoding the transformation expressions, the parser must be able to recognize file handling commands and respond to user inquiries. The parsing routines never call `getchar()` but use `lex()` for all input. The routine `parse()` itself is called from the `main()` procedure repeatedly, until it returns `false` (a value of zero):

```
main()
{
        ...
        do noerr=1; while( parse() );
}
```

The variable `noerr` is used as an error flag that is reset each time the parse routine is called. But more about error handling later. The parser will return zero only on an explicit `quit` command `q` from the user.

```
parse()
{       extern int lat;          /* look ahead token */

        printf("-> ");
        while (noerr)
        {       switch (lat = lex()) {
                case  'q': return 0;
                case '\n': return 1;
                case  ';': break;
                case  'f': showfiles();
                           break;
                case  'r': getname();
                           if (!noerr) continue;
                           getpix(&src[nsrc], text);
                           break;
                case  'w': getname();
                           if (!noerr) continue;
                           putpix(&src[CUROLD], text);
                           break;
                default  : transform();
                           if (noerr) run();
                           break;
        }       }
}
```

The parser indicates its willingness to accept a new command from the user by printing a prompt `->` with the I/O routine `printf(string)`. The routine `printf()` is used in two flavors here. As shown, it just prints text on the user's screen, possibly with some extra arguments for printing numbers and character strings. We will also use it as `fprintf(stderr,string)` to print error messages. (If your system has no separate channel for error messages, they can equally well be printed with `printf(string)`.)

Commands are typed on a single line separated by semicolons, or on separate lines. If the command can be parsed without syntax errors, the transformation program built by the parser is executed by the interpreter. This *program* is in reality a sequence of tokens (numbers) stored in an array called `parsed[]`. Below, this is referred to as the *parse string*. For completeness, here is also the routine `getname()` that is used in `parse()` to fetch a filename argument (a single alphanumeric character, or one of the tokens `FNAME` or `NAME` with a string attribute).

```
getname()
{       int t = lex();

        if (t != NAME && t != FNAME && !isalpha(t))
                error("expected name, bad token: %d\n", t);
}
```

`error()` is the routine to be called when a syntax error is detected. It will eat up the rest of the input, up to a newline, and set an error flag that will avoid the interpreter from being run on erroneous input.

```
error(s, d)
        char *s;
{
        extern int lat;

        fprintf(stderr, s, d);
        while (lat != '\n')
                lat = lex();
        noerr = 0;        /* noerr is now false */
}
```

Having seen the lexical analyzer and the main routine of the parser, you already know almost everything there is to know about the working of *popi*. We only have to fill in a few details, such as the parsing of expressions, the execution of parse strings and the reading and writing of image files.

Grammar Rules

When the parser starts processing a transformation expression it expects to see a sequence such as

```
new[x,y] = expression.
```

This sequence reaches the parser as a token `NEW` followed by a character `[`, an expression for the `x` index, a comma, another expression for the `y`, a character =, and a final expression for the values to be assigned. As an added difficulty we will allow for certain standard parts of this sequence to be omitted. The editor should be able to fill in the missing parts with defaults. For instance, if the index to array `new` is missing, as in

```
new = expression
```

the parser may assume a default index `[x,y]`. If the token `new` is also missing, and the statement just reads

```
expression
```

the parser can assume that you meant an assignment to image array `new` with the default index `[x,y]`.

To make more precise what type of expressions are acceptable to the parser, we define a grammar. A transformation, for instance, takes one of three possible forms, which we can describe as follows:

```
trans   →       NEW `[' index `]' `=' expr
        |       NEW `=' expr
        |       expr
```

This grammar rule is called a *production*. On the left-hand side of the arrow we write the name of the phrase or language fragment we want to define. Here we wrote `trans`, as an abbreviation of "transformation expression." The right-hand side shows a number of alternative ways in which the phrase can be constructed. The alternatives are separated by vertical bars. Quoted characters are called *literals*, and names in capitals are called *terminals*. Everything in a production except the literals and terminals must be expanded in still other productions, so that eventually everything can be defined recursively in terms of literals and terminals only. Note that the lexical analyzer we discussed before will recognize all the literals and terminals for us, and pass them as tokens to the parser.

The only undefined term in the production above is `expr`. So we will have to define it.

```
expr    →       term
        |       term `?' expr `:' expr
```

This rule says that an expression is either a conditional expression or something called a `term`. Note that conditional expressions can have other conditionals inside, but not in the term before the question mark.

```
term    →       factor binop term
```

This time we have two nonterminals in the production: `binop` and `factor`. The expansion for `binop`, or binary operator, is quickly defined.

```
binop   →       `*' | `/' | `%'
        |       `+' | `-'
        |       `>' | `<' | GE | LE | EQ | NE
        |       `^' | AND | OR
```

A `factor` is a little more work.

```
factor  →       `(' expr `)'
        |       `-' factor
        |       `!' factor
        |       OLD
        |       fileref
        |       value
        |       `x'
        |       `y'
        |       factor POW factor
```

A factor, then, can be any expression enclosed in parentheses; it may be preceded by a single minus sign (the unary minus) or a single exclamation mark (a boolean negation). It can be the token `OLD`, the characters `x` and `y`, or a `factor` raised to the power of some other `factor`. It can also be a constant value or a file reference `fileref`. This nonterminal, in turn, can be defined as follows:

```
fileref →        FNAME
        ¦        FNAME `[' index `]'
        ¦        `$' value
        ¦        `$' value `[' index ']'
```

$FNAME$ is the token returned by the lexical analyzer when it recognizes the name of an open image file in the input. We allow for file references to be either symbolic (e.g., `pjw[x,y]`) or numeric (as in `$1[x,y]`). The correspondence between names and numbers is given by the `f` command, discussed earlier. This leaves only the following nonterminals to be expanded.

```
value    →       digit ¦ digit value
index    →       expr `,' expr
```

and trivially:

```
digit    →       `0' ¦ `1' ¦ `2' ¦ `3' ¦ `4'
         ¦       `5' ¦ `6' ¦ `7' ¦ `8' ¦ `9'
```

Now let's look at the code for the parser that makes it all happen. The parser's job is to read the transformation expressions, flag syntax errors, and build a program for the interpreter that encodes the expressions.

The treatment of the defaults requires some attention. Remember that each image buffer takes either an explicit, user-defined index or, if the user omits it, an implicit index `[x,y]`. If the index to the destination buffer `new` is omitted, the parser inserts a special symbol `@` into the program to tell the interpreter to use the default index and destination, i.e., `new[x,y]`. The processing of explicit or implicit indexes to image files stored in other image buffers is deferred to a procedure named `fileref()`.

Here, first, is the code for routine `transform()`, that is called from `parse()` at the start of a transformation expression.

```
transform()
{       extern int prs;

        prs = 0; /* initial length of parse string */
        if (lat != NEW)
        {       expr();
                emit('@');
                pushback(lat);
                return;
        }
        lat = lex();
        if (lat == '[')
        {       fileref(CURNEW, LVAL);
                expect('='); expr(); emit('=');
        } else
        {       expect('='); expr(); emit('@');
        }
```

```
            if (lat != '\n' && lat != ';')
                    error("syntax error, separator\n");
            pushback(lat);
    }
```

The symbol @ is really an abstract instruction of the stack machine that runs the transformations. An assignment to any other location in array **new** is encoded with an explicit "instruction" =. The program for the interpreter, or the *parse string* as we have called it before, is built in an array called parsed. We use a procedure **emit(symbol)** to add new symbols to the parse string.

```
    emit(what)
    {
            if (prs >= MANY)
                    error("expression too long\n");
            parsed[prs++] = what;
    }
```

The parse string is in standard postfix notation, with a few special operators such as @ and =. In postfix notation the expression **new=x**y** becomes '**x, y, POW, @**.' The operators simply follow the operands to which they apply, instead of sitting between them. This format greatly simplifies the design of the interpreter. Procedure **expect(token)** checks that the look-ahead token **lat** matches the expected value and then reads in the next token from the lexical analyzer.

```
    expect(t)
    {
            if (lat == t)
                    lat = lex();
            else
                    error("error: expected token %d\n",t);
    }
```

fileref() is a procedure that decodes a reference to an image buffer. It has to check that the image is really available, and it must properly decode the index. A file reference can occur in two different contexts: on the left-hand side or the right-hand side of an assignment. In the first case the interpreter will have to calculate the address of the location in the destination buffer where a new pixel value is to be stored; in the second case it simply needs to read a pixel value from that location and can forget about its address. The parser will distinguish the two different uses by using either the symbol **LVAL** or **RVAL** in the second argument to **fileref()**. As it turns out, we will only allow array **new** to be used as an **LVAL**. Here is the code. The appropriate token value to be issued is passed as in argument **tok** (see, for instance, the usage of **fileref()** in the **transform()** routine above).

```
fileref(val, tok)
{
        if (val < 0 || val >= nsrc)
                error("bad file number: %d\n", val);

        emit(VALUE);
        emit(val);
        if (lat == '[')
        {       lat = lex();
                expr(); expect(',');
                expr(); expect(']');    /* [x,y] */
        } else
        {       emit('x');
                emit('y');
        }
        emit(tok);
}
```

A value is encoded in the parse string by the symbol **VALUE** followed by the actual number seen.

More about Parsing Expressions

The most important part of the parser starts with **expr()**. It is time to worry here about operator precedence rules. An expression like **512*y+x** is to be interpreted as **(512*y)+x** instead of **512*(y+x)**. In postfix form this is the difference between parsing 512,y,*,x,+ and 512,y,x,+,*. To ensure that the parser gives multiplications, divisions, and modulo operations a higher priority than, for instance, additions or subtractions, we use a lookup table that encodes four precedence levels.

```
int op[4][7] = {
        { '*', '/', '%', 0, 0, 0, 0, },
        { '+', '-',  0, 0, 0, 0, 0, },
        { '>', '<', GE, LE, EQ, NE, 0, },
        { '^', AND, OR, 0, 0, 0, 0, },
};
```

Procedure **expr()** uses a generic procedure **level(nr)** to parse subexpressions for precedence level **nr**. It tries to parse the highest-precedence operators first. At the highest level it tries to find a **factor()** such as a number or a variable. At the other levels it checks for the appropriate operators in the table shown above. The lowest level is given to the operators of a conditional expression (a question mark and a colon).

```
expr()
{       extern int prs;
        extern int parsed[MANY];
        int rememl, remem2;

        level(3);
        if (lat == '?')
        {       lat = lex();
                emit('?');
                rememl = prs; emit(0);
                expr();
                expect(':'); emit(':');
                remem2 = prs; emit(0);
                parsed[rememl] = prs-1;
                expr();
                parsed[remem2] = prs-1;
        }
}
```

Conditional image transformation commands are built from three sub-expressions:

`condition?iftrue:iffalse`.

If, at runtime, the condition is found to be true, the interpreter will execute the instructions in array `parsed` for the `iftrue` part. If, however, the condition is found to be false, the interpreter should be able to skip to the `iffalse` part. To allow the interpreter to do this at runtime, the parser reserves a slot in the parse string for the destination of the jump. The slot is filled with that destination after the colon has been parsed. Similarly, after executing an `iftrue` part, the interpreter must skip to the end of the conditional. Again the proper destination can be patched into the string, but only after the end of the `iffalse` expression has been seen (i.e., a semicolon or a newline).

```
level(nr)
{       int i;
        extern int noerr;

        if (nr < 0)
        {       factor();
                return;
        }
        level(nr-1);
        for (i = 0; op[nr][i] != 0 && noerr; i++)
                if (lat == op[nr][i])
                {       lat = lex();
                        level(nr);
                        emit(op[nr][i]);
                        break;
                }
}
```

A factor, finally, is defined as follows:

```
factor()
{       int n;

        switch (lat) {
        case   '(':      lat = lex();
                         expr();
                         expect(')');
                         break;
        case   '-':      lat = lex();
                         factor();
                         emit(UMIN);
                         break;
        case   '!':      lat = lex();
                         factor();
                         emit('!');
                         break;
        case   OLD:      lat = lex();
                         fileref(CUROLD, RVAL);
                         break;
        case FNAME:      n = lexval;
                         lat = lex();
                         fileref(n+1, RVAL);
                         break;
        case   '$':      lat = lex();
                         expect(VALUE);
                         fileref(lexval+1, RVAL);
                         break;
        case VALUE:      emit(VALUE);
                         emit(lexval);
                         lat = lex();
                         break;
        case 'y':
        case 'x':        emit(lat);
                         lat = lex();
                         break;
        default :        error("expr: syntax error\n");
        }
        if (lat == POW)
        {       lat = lex();
                factor();
                emit(POW);
        }
}
```

In the order listed, a factor can be an expression enclosed in parentheses, a factor preceded by a minus sign (unary minus), or a logical negation. It can also be a symbolic or a numeric file reference, a value, a Cartesian coordinate, or a factor raised to some other factor with a power operator.

So far, we have discussed the lexical analyzer and the parser. The interpreter and the file handler remain to be discussed. Before we discuss the file handler, first a few words about the specific data structures that are used for storing the images.

Data Structure

Images are stored in a structure of the following type:

```
struct SRC {
        char *str;                  /* file name    */
        unsigned char **pix;        /* pixel values */
} src[];
```

The format is one byte per pixel, `DEF_X` pixels per scanline, and `DEF_Y` scanlines per image. We will use two of these structures as edit buffers: `src[0]` and `src[1]` with `DEF_Y`×`DEF_X` pixels. The result of the last edit operation is in one of these two arrays and is referred to as `old`. Internally, it is addressed as `src[CUROLD].pix`. Similarly, the destination of an edit operation is in the other edit buffer named `new`, or `src[CURNEW].pix`.

The default image resolution is defined by two constants:

```
#define DEF_X   248
#define DEF_Y   248
```

What follows is an aside on the choice of the resolution, which you can skip on a first reading:

> The precise value you can afford to enter for `DEF_X` and `DEF_Y` depends on the amount of memory in your computer and the type of memory allocation performed. On most systems, an image size of 248×248 will allow for a generous number of image files to be open for editing simultaneously. Smaller computers, that is, computers with a wordsize of 16 instead of 32 or 64 bits, can make it hard to allocate more than 2^{16} = 64k bytes at a time. We therefore chose to allocate memory for the images in increments of `DEF_X`, once for each scanline, instead of once for each picture.
>
> A few more hairy details. An allocator sometimes uses a few bytes from each block allocated for its own housekeeping. On a small system, this makes it attractive to pick a value for `DEF_X` that is the same number of bytes smaller than a power of 2 so that we can evenly fill up available memory, without leaving gaps. (The amount of real memory available comes in powers of 2.) In this case we chose 256 − 8=248, which turns out to be an good size for an AT&T PC6300+ system running UNIX. On a larger system you need not worry about memory allocation details and just select any frame size that is convenient to work with.

File Handler

We need routines to read and write image files, and to show which files are currently open. The last one is easy:

```
showfiles()
{       int n;

        if (nsrc == 2)
                printf("no files open\n");
        else
                for (n = 2; n < nsrc; n++)
                        printf("$%d = %s\n", n-1, src[n].str);
}
```

It uses `printf()` again, this time with two extra arguments: a number to be printed at the place indicated with `%d` and a name to be printed at the `%s`.

Reading new files, including the required memory allocation, can be done as follows, using the standard I/O routines `fopen()`, `fread()`, and `fclose()`. A call to `fopen(str,"r")` opens the file named `str` for reading. Similarly `fopen(str,"w")` opens the file for writing, and creates it if it does not exist. `fread(ptr,n,m,fd)` reads `m` chunks of `n` bytes from the file referred to by file descriptor `fd` and places it at the location given by `ptr`.

```
getpix(into, str)
        struct SRC *into;       /* work buffer */
        char *str;              /* file name   */
{
        FILE *fd;
        int i;

        if ((fd = fopen(str, "r")) == NULL)
        {       fprintf(stderr, "no file %s\n", str);
                return;
        }

        if (into->pix == (unsigned char **) 0)
        {       into->pix = (unsigned char **)
                        Emalloc(DEF_Y * sizeof(unsigned char *));
                for (i = 0; i < DEF_Y; i++)
                        into->pix[i] = (unsigned char *)
                                Emalloc(DEF_X);
        }
        into->str = (char *) Emalloc(strlen(str)+1);
        if (!noerr) return;     /* set by Emalloc */

        for (i = 0; i < DEF_Y; i++)
                fread(into->pix[i], 1, DEF_X, fd);
        strcpy(into->str, str);

        fclose(fd);
        nsrc++;
}
```

A separate procedure is used to access the memory allocator, to make it easier to catch errors:

```
char *
Emalloc(N)
{       char *try, *malloc();

        if ((try = malloc(N)) == NULL)
                error("out of memory\n");
        return try;
}
```

Writing files is also simple. `fwrite(ptr,n,m,fd)` writes `m` chunks of data, of `n` bytes each, from a location pointed to by `ptr` into the file with descriptor `fd`.

```
putpix(into, str)
        struct SRC *into;       /* work buffer */
        char *str;              /* file name   */
{
        FILE *fd;
        int i;

        if ((fd = fopen(str, "w")) == NULL)
        {       fprintf(stderr, "cannot create %s\n", str);
                return;
        }
        for (i = 0; i < DEF_Y; i++)
                fwrite(into->pix[i], 1, DEF_X, fd);
        fclose(fd);
}
```

The Interpreter

The interpreter is a sensitive piece of code since it is asked to execute the parse string once for every pixel in the image being edited. Even for a small image size of 248×248 pixels the interpreter must run through the parse string 61,504 times. It is important that it is as fast as it can be.

The interpreter is built as a *stack* machine. It maintains a pointer `rr` to a stack of values. Values and variables are pushed onto the stack. Operators and functions pop the stack and replace the values at the top with their result. At the end of each run of the interpreter that stack should be empty. The runtime stack contains *long* values instead of *integers* to allow for the computation of both pixel values and pixel addresses.

For convenience we define a macro `dop(OP)` for the frequently occurring operation that pops two values from the stack, applies an operation `OP` to them, and then pushes the result back.

```
#define dop(OP) a = *--rr; tr = rr-1; *tr = (*tr OP (long)a)
```

Variable `rr` points to the first free slot on the stack. The topmost symbol on the stack is at position `(rr−1)`. The `dop` macro can be used for all binary arithmetic and boolean operations. The interpreter will keep a pointer to the default destination of pixel assignments up to date in a pointer `p`.

```
run()
{       long R[MANY];                  /* the stack      */
        register long *rr, *tr;        /* top of stack */
        register unsigned char *u; /* explicit destination */
        register unsigned char *p; /* default  destination */
        register int k;                /* indexes parse string */
        int a, b, c;                   /* scratch        */
        int x, y;                      /* coordinates */

        p = src[CURNEW].pix[0];
        for (y = 0; y < DEF_Y; y++, p = src[CURNEW].pix[y])
        for (x = 0; x < DEF_X; x++, p++)
        for (k = 0, rr = R; k < prs; k++)
        {       if (parsed[k] == VALUE)
                {       *rr++ = (long)parsed[++k];
                        continue;
                }
                if (parsed[k] == '@')
                {       *p = (unsigned char) (*--rr);
                        continue;
                }
                switch (parsed[k]) {
                case  '+': dop(+);  break;
                case  '-': dop(-);  break;
                case  '*': dop(*);  break;
                case  '/': dop(/);  break;
                case  '%': dop(%);  break;
                case  '>': dop(>);  break;
                case  '<': dop(<);  break;
                case   GE: dop(>=); break;
                case   LE: dop(<=); break;
                case   EQ: dop(==); break;
                case   NE: dop(!=); break;
                case  AND: dop(&&); break;
                case   OR: dop(||); break;
                case  '^': dop(|);  break;
                case  'x': *rr++ = (long)x; break;
                case  'y': *rr++ = (long)y; break;
                case UMIN: tr = rr-1; *tr = -(*tr); break;
                case  '!': tr = rr-1; *tr = !(*tr); break;
                case  '=': a = *--rr;
                           u = (unsigned char *) *--rr;
                           *u = (unsigned char) a;
                           break;
                case RVAL: a = *--rr;
                           b = *--rr;
                           tr = rr-1;
                           c = *tr;
                           *tr = (long) src[c].pix[a][b];
                           break;
```

```
                    case LVAL: a = *--rr;
                               b = *--rr;
                               tr = rr-1;
                               c = *tr;
                               *tr = (long) &(src[c].pix[a][b]);
                               break;
                    case  POW: a = *--rr;
                               *(rr-1) = Pow(*(rr-1),(long)a);
                               break;
                    case  '?': a = *--rr; k++;
                               if (!a) k = parsed[k];
                               break;
                    case  ':': k = parsed[k+1]; break;

                    default  : error("run: unknown operator\n");
                    }
          }
          CUROLD = CURNEW; CURNEW = 1-CUROLD;
}
```

It may look curious that two of the "instructions" are processed before the large case switch is entered. They catch the two most frequently executed operations and it makes the interpreter run faster to process them first. At the end of the run the two edit buffers, referred to by `old` and `new`, are swapped. Note that the procedure `Pow()` accepts and returns *long* values. To make use of the *C* library routine, you can define

```
long
Pow(a, b)
          long a, b;
{         double c = (double)a;
          double d = (double)b;
          return (long) pow(c, d);
}
```

The Complete Program

Here, finally, is the complete listing of the program, with all loose ends neatly tied up. On a UNIX system it is compiled with the command

```
cc -o popi main.c lex.c io.c expr.c run.c
```

If `display` is the name of a display routine that can show an unformatted image file on the specific monitor you use, you can test the working of the editor with the commands.

```
$ popi              invoke the editor
-> x^y              create a test pattern
-> w test           write it in a file
-> q                quit the editor
display test        display the result
```

Try it. You'll like it.

```
/***  popi.h (header file) **************************/

#define MANY    128
#define DEF_X   248     /* image width  */
#define DEF_Y   248     /* image height */

#define RVAL    257     /* larger than any char token */
#define LVAL    258
#define FNAME   259
#define VALUE   260
#define NAME    261
#define NEW     262
#define OLD     263
#define AND     264
#define OR      265
#define EQ      266
#define NE      267
#define GE      268
#define LE      269
#define UMIN    270
#define POW     271

struct SRC {
        unsigned char **pix;    /* pix[y][x] */
        char *str;
};

/***  main.c ***************************************/

#include        <stdio.h>
#include        <ctype.h>
#include        "popi.h"

int     parsed[MANY];
struct  SRC     src[MANY];
short   CUROLD=0, CURNEW=1;
int     noerr, lexval, prs=0, nsrc=2;
char    text[256];

char *Emalloc();

main(argc, argv)
        char **argv;
{
        int i;

        src[CUROLD].pix = (unsigned char **)
                Emalloc(DEF_Y * sizeof(unsigned char *));
        src[CURNEW].pix = (unsigned char **)
                Emalloc(DEF_Y * sizeof(unsigned char *));
```

```
        for (i = 0; i < DEF_Y; i++)
        {       src[CUROLD].pix[i] = (unsigned char *)
                        Emalloc(DEF_X);
                src[CURNEW].pix[i] = (unsigned char *)
                        Emalloc(DEF_X);
        }

        for (i = 1; i < argc; i++)
                getpix(&src[nsrc], argv[i]);

        do noerr=1; while( parse() );
}

parse()
{       extern int lat;         /* look ahead token */

        printf("-> ");
        while (noerr)
        {       switch (lat = lex()) {
                case  'q': return 0;
                case '\n': return 1;
                case  ';': break;
                case  'f': showfiles();
                           break;
                case  'r': getname();
                           if (!noerr) continue;
                           getpix(&src[nsrc], text);
                           break;
                case  'w': getname();
                           if (!noerr) continue;
                           putpix(&src[CUROLD], text);
                           break;
                default  : transform();
                           if (noerr) run();
                           break;
        }       }
}

getname()
{       int t = lex();

        if (t != NAME && t != FNAME && !isalpha(t))
                error("expected name, bad token: %d\n", t);
}

emit(what)
{
        if (prs >= MANY)
                error("expression too long\n");
        parsed[prs++] = what;
}
```

```
error(s, d)
        char *s;
{
        extern int lat;

        fprintf(stderr, s, d);
        while (lat != '\n')
                lat = lex();
        noerr = 0;        /* noerr is now false */
}

char *
Emalloc(N)
{       char *try, *malloc();

        if ((try = malloc(N)) == NULL)
                error("out of memory\n");
        return try;
}

/***  lex.c  (lexical analyzer) *********************/

#include <stdio.h>
#include <ctype.h>
#include "popi.h"

extern struct   SRC src[MANY];
extern short    CUROLD, CURNEW;
extern int      nsrc, lexval;
extern char     text[];

lex()
{       int c;

        do      /* ignore white space */
                c = getchar();
        while (c == ' ' || c == '\t');

        if (isdigit(c))
                c = getnumber(c);
        else if (isalpha(c) || c == '_')
                c = getstring(c);
```

```
        switch (c) {
        case EOF:  c = 'q'; break;
        case '*':  c = follow('*', POW, c); break;
        case '>':  c = follow('=', GE,  c); break;
        case '<':  c = follow('=', LE,  c); break;
        case '!':  c = follow('=', NE,  c); break;
        case '=':  c = follow('=', EQ,  c); break;
        case '|':  c = follow('|', OR,  c); break;
        case '&':  c = follow('&', AND, c); break;
        case 'Z':  c = VALUE; lexval = 255; break;
        case 'Y':  c = VALUE; lexval = DEF_Y-1; break;
        case 'X':  c = VALUE; lexval = DEF_X-1; break;
        default :  break;
        }
        return c;
}

getnumber(first)
{       int c;

        lexval = first - '0';
        while (isdigit(c = getchar()))
                lexval = 10*lexval + c - '0';
        pushback(c);
        return VALUE;
}

getstring(first)
{       int c = first;
        char *str = text;

        do {
                *str++ = c;
                c = getchar();
        } while (isalpha(c) || c == '_' || isdigit(c));
        *str = '\0';
        pushback(c);

        if (strcmp(text, "new") == 0) return NEW;
        if (strcmp(text, "old") == 0) return OLD;

        for (c = 2; c < nsrc; c++)
                if (strcmp(src[c].str, text) == 0)
                {       lexval = c-1;
                        return FNAME;
                }
        if (strlen(text) > 1)
                return NAME;
        return first;
}
```

```
follow(tok, ifyes, ifno)
{       int c;

        if ((c = getchar()) == tok)
                return ifyes;
        pushback(c);

        return ifno;
}

pushback(c)
{
        ungetc(c, stdin);
}

/***  io.c   (file handler)  ************************/

#include        <stdio.h>
#include        "popi.h"

extern struct SRC src[MANY];
extern int nsrc, noerr;
extern char *Emalloc();

getpix(into, str)
        struct SRC *into;       /* work buffer */
        char *str;              /* file name   */
{
        FILE *fd;
        int i;

        if ((fd = fopen(str, "r")) == NULL)
        {       fprintf(stderr, "no file %s\n", str);
                return;
        }

        if (into->pix == (unsigned char **) 0)
        {       into->pix = (unsigned char **)
                        Emalloc(DEF_Y * sizeof(unsigned char *));
                for (i = 0; i < DEF_Y; i++)
                        into->pix[i] = (unsigned char *)
                                Emalloc(DEF_X);
        }
        into->str = (char *) Emalloc(strlen(str)+1);
        if (!noerr) return;     /* set by Emalloc */

        for (i = 0; i < DEF_Y; i++)
                fread(into->pix[i], 1, DEF_X, fd);
        strcpy(into->str, str);

        fclose(fd);
        nsrc++;
}
```

```
putpix(into, str)
        struct SRC *into;         /* work buffer */
        char *str;                /* file name   */
{
        FILE *fd;
        int i;

        if ((fd = fopen(str, "w")) == NULL)
        {       fprintf(stderr, "cannot create %s\n", str);
                return;
        }
        for (i = 0; i < DEF_Y; i++)
                fwrite(into->pix[i], 1, DEF_X, fd);
        fclose(fd);
}

showfiles()
{       int n;

        if (nsrc == 2)
                printf("no files open\n");
        else
                for (n = 2; n < nsrc; n++)
                        printf("$%d = %s\n", n-1, src[n].str);
}

/***  expr.c (parser)  ******************************/

#include "popi.h"

extern int      lexval, nsrc;
extern struct   SRC     src[MANY];
extern short    CUROLD, CURNEW;
int             lat;    /* look ahead token */

int op[4][7] = {
        { '*', '/', '%', 0, 0, 0, 0, },
        { '+', '-',   0, 0, 0, 0, 0, },
        { '>', '<',  GE, LE, EQ, NE, 0, },
        { '^', AND,  OR, 0, 0, 0, 0, },
};
```

```
expr()
{       extern int prs;
        extern int parsed[MANY];
        int remem1, remem2;

        level(3);
        if (lat == '?')
        {       lat = lex();
                emit('?');
                remem1 = prs; emit(0);
                expr();
                expect(':'); emit(':');
                remem2 = prs; emit(0);
                parsed[remem1] = prs-1;
                expr();
                parsed[remem2] = prs-1;
        }
}

level(nr)
{       int i;
        extern int noerr;

        if (nr < 0)
        {       factor();
                return;
        }
        level(nr-1);
        for (i = 0; op[nr][i] != 0 && noerr; i++)
                if (lat == op[nr][i])
                {       lat = lex();
                        level(nr);
                        emit(op[nr][i]);
                        break;
                }
}

transform()
{       extern int prs;

        prs = 0; /* initial length of parse string */
        if (lat != NEW)
        {       expr();
                emit('@');
                pushback(lat);
                return;
        }
```

```
        lat = lex();
        if (lat == '[')
        {       fileref(CURNEW, LVAL);
                expect('='); expr(); emit('=');
        } else
        {       expect('='); expr(); emit('@');
        }
        if (lat != '\n' && lat != ';')
                error("syntax error, separator\n");
        pushback(lat);
}

factor()
{       int n;

        switch (lat) {
        case   '(':     lat = lex();
                        expr();
                        expect(')');
                        break;
        case   '-':     lat = lex();
                        factor();
                        emit(UMIN);
                        break;
        case   '!':     lat = lex();
                        factor();
                        emit('!');
                        break;
        case   OLD:     lat = lex();
                        fileref(CUROLD, RVAL);
                        break;
        case FNAME:     n = lexval;
                        lat = lex();
                        fileref(n+1, RVAL);
                        break;
        case   '$':     lat = lex();
                        expect(VALUE);
                        fileref(lexval+1, RVAL);
                        break;
        case VALUE:     emit(VALUE);
                        emit(lexval);
                        lat = lex();
                        break;
        case 'y':
        case 'x':       emit(lat);
                        lat = lex();
                        break;
        default :       error("expr: syntax error\n");
        }
```

```
		if (lat == POW)
		{	lat = lex();
			factor();
			emit(POW);
		}
}

fileref(val, tok)
{
		if (val < 0 || val >= nsrc)
			error("bad file number: %d\n", val);

		emit(VALUE);
		emit(val);
		if (lat == '[')
		{	lat = lex();
			expr(); expect(',');
			expr(); expect(']');	/* [x,y] */
		} else
		{	emit('x');
			emit('y');
		}
		emit(tok);
}

expect(t)
{
		if (lat == t)
			lat = lex();
		else
			error("error: expected token %d\n",t);
}

/***  run.c  (interpreter) **************************/

#include	"popi.h"

extern int	prs, parsed[MANY];
extern struct	SRC	src[MANY];
extern short	CUROLD, CURNEW;

#define dop(OP) a = *--rr; tr = rr-1; *tr = (*tr OP (long)a)

long
Pow(a, b)
		long a, b;
{
		double c = (double)a;
		double d = (double)b;
		double pow();

		return (long) pow(c, d);
}
```

```
run()
{       long R[MANY];                   /* the stack     */
        register long *rr, *tr;         /* top of stack */
        register unsigned char *u;      /* explicit destination */
        register unsigned char *p;      /* default  destination */
        register int k;                 /* indexes parse string */
        int a, b, c;                    /* scratch       */
        int x, y;                       /* coordinates */

        p = src[CURNEW].pix[0];
        for (y = 0; y < DEF_Y; y++, p = src[CURNEW].pix[y])
        for (x = 0; x < DEF_X; x++, p++)
        for (k = 0, rr = R; k < prs; k++)
        {       if (parsed[k] == VALUE)
                {       *rr++ = (long)parsed[++k];
                        continue;
                }
                if (parsed[k] == '@')
                {       *p = (unsigned char) (*--rr);
                        continue;
                }
                switch (parsed[k]) {
                case  '+': dop(+);  break;
                case  '-': dop(-);  break;
                case  '*': dop(*);  break;
                case  '/': dop(/);  break;
                case  '%': dop(%);  break;
                case  '>': dop(>);  break;
                case  '<': dop(<);  break;
                case   GE: dop(>=); break;
                case   LE: dop(<=); break;
                case   EQ: dop(==); break;
                case   NE: dop(!=); break;
                case  AND: dop(&&); break;
                case   OR: dop(||); break;
                case  '^': dop(|);  break;
                case  'x': *rr++ = (long)x; break;
                case  'y': *rr++ = (long)y; break;
                case UMIN: tr = rr-1; *tr = -(*tr); break;
                case  '!': tr = rr-1; *tr = !(*tr); break;
                case  '=': a = *--rr;
                           u = (unsigned char *) *--rr;
                           *u = (unsigned char) a;
                           break;
                case RVAL: a = *--rr;
                           b = *--rr;
                           tr = rr-1;
                           c = *tr;
                           *tr = (long) src[c].pix[a][b];
                           break;
```

```
                case LVAL: a = *--rr;
                           b = *--rr;
                           tr = rr-1;
                           c = *tr;
                           *tr = (long) &(src[c].pix[a][b]);
                           break;
                case  POW: a = *--rr;
                           *(rr-1) = Pow(*(rr-1),(long)a);
                           break;
                case  '?': a = *--rr; k++;
                           if (!a) k = parsed[k];
                           break;
                case  ':': k = parsed[k+1]; break;

                default  : error("run: unknown operator\n");
                }
        }
        CUROLD = CURNEW; CURNEW = 1-CUROLD;
}
```

Library Routines

Here is an overview of the library routines that were used in the program. It should not be hard to find equivalents for them if you run on a system other than UNIX. They are all considered standard routines in the *C* programming language.

fclose	fread	isalpha	pow	strcpy
fopen	fwrite	isdigit	printf	strlen
fprintf	getchar	malloc	strcmp	ungetc

Efficiency Considerations

The complete program listed above is only about 500 lines of *C* text. Yet it can be an amazingly powerful package once you get the hang of the notation for transformation expressions. I have run it under a UNIX operating system on an AT&T PC6300+, a DEC VAX/750, a DEC VAX/785, and a CRAY/XMP computer. Not to worry, the difference in performance for the software is not nearly as spectacular as the difference in price of this hardware. Here is a comparison of runtimes for a few transformations. All times given are in seconds.

Runtimes (frame size: 248×248 pixels)

Transformation	PC6300+	VAX/750	VAX/785	CRAY/XMP
new=128	7.2	4.1	1.6	0.1
new=pjw	24.2	10.5	3.7	0.4
new=Z-old	32.4	15.1	5.2	0.6
new=(pjw+rob)/2	59.2	25.9	9.7	1.0
new=(x<X/2)?pjw:rob	63.1	33.2	13.9	1.4
new=(pjw<128)?Z-pjw:pjw[X-x,y]	79.3	38.6	14.8	1.6

The times quoted are for the program as listed, with interpreted code. Since the interpreter runs the same code many thousands of times, even for a single image transformation, every improvement in that portion of the code pays off immediately. One way to achieve a substantial speedup is to replace the interpreter with an on-the-fly compiler that translates the transformation program into machine code and runs it. It will go too far to get into the details of that extension, but suffice it to say that it is worth the effort. The speed difference between interpreted code and compiled code can be as high as 1:100 for nontrivial transformations. The program *popi* you see above is a predecessor of the image editor called *pico*. *Pico* has the same basic structure as *popi*, but has the built-in compiler to make it faster. The compiler extension more than doubles the size of the program, but in a way it can achieve the same as the purchase of a Cray supercomputer. (The performance of running *pico* with compiled code on a Cray is of course utterly decadent.)

Adding a Display Routine

To display an image on your terminal screen requires code that is hardware dependent, so I have not included it in *popi*, but you can easily extend the software in this way. If you have a one-byte-per-pixel monitor, you can write the pixel values to the screen without processing.

```
display(pix)
        unsigned char **pix;
{
        register int x, y;

        for (y = 0; y < DEF_Y; y++)
        for (x = 0; x < DEF_X; x++)
                putdot(pix[y][x], x, y);
}
```

The device-dependent routine `putdot(val,x,y)` should write a pixel with brightness `val` at location `x,y` on the screen. Note, however, that most display monitors will work substantially faster if you can write one scanline at a time, using, for example:

```
        for (y = 0; y < DEF_Y; y++)
                putline(pix[y], y);
```

Some display monitors use a different type of coordinate system, e.g., with `Y` at the top of the screen and 0 at the bottom. You can use the same routine, and simply subtract the `y` variable from `Y` to produce a picture that is right side up:

```
        for (y = 0; y < DEF_Y; y++)
                putline(pix[y], DEF_Y-1-y);
```

If you have a one-bit-per-pixel dot-mapped monitor, the image has to be halftoned before it can be displayed. Here is a routine that you can use. It uses a standard halftoning method, like the ones used for printing photos in newspapers, to map gray values onto pure black-and-white values. (For more information on halftoning methods, refer to the bibliography at the end of this chapter.)

```
#define RES      8

thresh[RES][RES] = {
        {  0, 128,  32, 160,   8, 136,  40, 168, },
        {192,  64, 224,  96, 200,  72, 232, 104, },
        { 48, 176,  16, 144,  56, 184,  24, 152, },
        {240, 112, 208,  80, 248, 120, 216,  88, },
        { 12, 140,  44, 172,   4, 132,  36, 164, },
        {204,  76, 236, 108, 196,  68, 228, 100, },
        { 60, 188,  28, 156,  52, 180,  20, 148, },
        {252, 124, 220,  92, 244, 116, 212,  84, },
};      /* an array with threshold values */

display(pix)
        unsigned char **pix;
{
        register int x, y;

        for (y = 0; y < DEF_SZ; y++)
        for (x = 0; x < DEF_SZ; x++)
        {       if (pix[y][x] >= thresh[y%RES][x%RES])
                        putdot(1, x, y);
                else
                        putdot(0, x, y);
        }
}
```

Note again that it may be faster first to assemble a whole scanline of one bit dots in memory and write it to the screen with a single procedure call **putline()**.

Including the display routine in the editor is done in three steps. First, extend the lexical analyzer to recognize a new keyword, such as **display**, and return a new token, e.g., **DISP**. Then add a value for the new token to the header file "popi.h," e.g.,

```
#define DISP    272
```

Finally, extend the routine **parse()** to respond to the new command, by adding another case to the switch statement. For instance,

```
case DISP: display(src[CUROLD].pix); break;
```

If you are more daring, you want to consider including routine **putline()** directly inside **run()**. The best place to do this is at the end of the loop on variable **y**. The extra procedure call makes the program run a little slower. Being able to see the effect of a transformation happen in real-time, however, will more than make up for it.

In a similar way *popi* can be extended with any number of user-defined routines, either standard transformations that you would like to have predefined, or transformations that may be hard to express in the language of the transformation expressions. In Chapter 6 we include some examples of routines you may want to add in this manner.

Hints for Other Extensions

One of the first things you may want to do is to extend *popi* to handle both color and black-and-white images. One simple way to do this is to store pixel values not in 8-bit bytes but in 32-bit words (for instance, a long integer). You will need 8 bits each for the red, green, and blue color components, and use the remaining 8 bits to separate the color components within the pixel word. You will have to be careful to get the image arithmetic to work right, especially to avoid overflow between neighboring color components. But it is not too hard to do. Another method is, of course, to store the red, green, and blue components in three separate image files and use the editor as is.

The extension for polar coordinates (Chapter 3) is relatively easy. The simplest method is to prepare two files with precomputed values of all `r` and `a` values. The editor loads the two files in memory, as if they were image files, and simply looks up each `r` and `a` value as needed, instead of computing them over and over on-the-fly. You will need to add two lines to the parsing routine `factor()`, to catch `r` and `a` in the same case statement that processes `x` and `y`. Then you will have to add a modest amount of code to the interpreter routine `run()` to look up the precomputed value for either `r` or `a`, given `x` and `y`. The code for `RVAL` in `run()` can serve as an example.

Trigonometric functions are also relatively easy to add. The lexical analyzer will need to recognize a few more character sequences, such as *sin*, *cos*, and *atan*. They can be translated into three new tokens and interpreted by `run()` similar to the token `POW`. Note, however, that the *sin* and *cos* functions return values between +1.0 and −1.0, while the editor works only with integers. A simple way around this is to have these functions return 1000 times their value, and to renormalize the results in the transformation expressions.

Adding an `undo` operation takes only one line of code, to be added to the case switch in routine `parse()` in main.c.

```
case 'u': CUROLD = CURNEW; CURNEW = 1-CUROLD; break;
```

Those who really want to experiment will also want to consider the extension of *popi* with variables, interactively defined functions, and explicit control flow statements. Each such extension will increase both the power and the size of the editor. But be warned: If you are not a skilled programmer when you begin with these extensions, you probably will be when you complete them.

Books

A couple of books may be helpful if you would like to work with the software discussed above. The best reference to the *C* programming language is still Kernighan and Ritchie's manual from 1978. A discussion of the draft ANSI standard *C* language can be found in Harbison and Steele's book. Much more about the design of parsers and lexical analyzer can be found in the famous *dragon* books by Aho and others. A wealth of information on *C* programming can also be found in Kernighan and Pike's book on UNIX. Read especially Chapter 8 on program development if you consider extending *popi*.

An excellent introduction to digital halftoning methods can be found in Robert Ulichney's book.

For completeness the list below also includes a reference to a paper published in the *AT&T Technical Journal* with more information on the structure of the picture editor *pico*, *popi*'s bigger brother.

The C Programming Language, Brian W. Kernighan and Dennis M. Ritchie, Prentice Hall, 1978, 2nd revised edition 1988, ISBN 0-13-110163-3.

C – A Reference Manual, Samual P. Harbison and Guy L. Steele Jr., Prentice-Hall, 2nd edition, 1987, ISBN 0-13-109802-0.

Compilers – Principles, Techniques and Tools, Al Aho, Ravi Sethi, and Jeff Ullman. Addison-Wesley, 1986, ISBN 0-201-10088-6.

The UNIX Programming Environment, Brian W. Kernighan and Rob Pike, Prentice-Hall, 1984, ISBN 0-13-937699-2.

Digital Halftoning, Robert Ulichney, The MIT Press, 1987, ISBN 0-262-21009-6.

"Pico – a Picture Editor," Gerard J. Holzmann, *AT&T Technical Journal*, Vol. 66, No. 2, 1987, pp. 2–13.

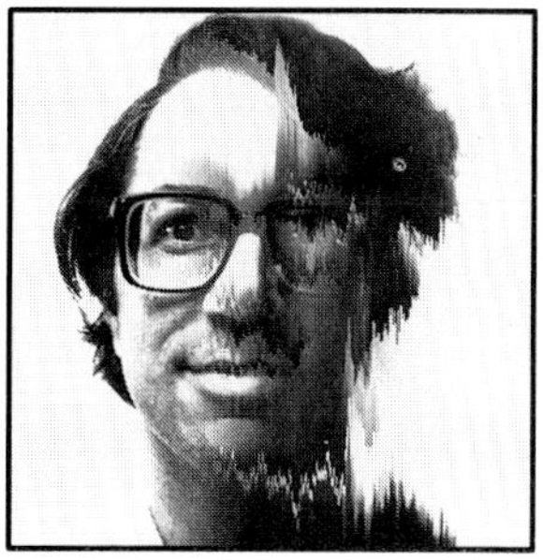

6 Catalogue of Transformations

We conclude with a list of image transformations in the picture language for *popi*. We make full use of the defaults for indexing, so `old[x,y]` is abbreviated to `old`, and a default assignment `new[x,y]=` is always omitted. Most of the transformations were illustrated in Chapters 3 and 4. At the completion of each command, or sequence of commands, listed here the edit buffer will contain the required image. The last few examples are transformations that are harder to express in *popi*, but that can be added as user-defined routines, as shown in Chapter 5 (see *Adding a Display Routine*).

Making a Negative

```
Z-old
```

Logarithmic Correction

```
Z*log(old)/log(Z)
```

Simulated Solarization

```
(old > Z/2) ? Z-old : old
```

Contrast Expansion and Normalization

```
(Z*(old-L))/(H-L)
```

Assumes brightness values in the range `L` to `H`.

Focus Restoration

```
5*old-old[x-1,y]-old[x+1,y]-old[x,y-1]-old[x,y+1]
```

Blurring

```
(old[x-2,y-2]+old[x-1,y-2]+old[x,y-2]+old[x+1,y-2]+
 old[x-2,y-1]+old[x-1,y-1]+old[x,y-1]+old[x+1,y-1]+
 old[x-2,y  ]+old[x-1,y  ]+old[x,y  ]+old[x+1,y  ]+
 old[x-2,y+1]+old[x-1,y+1]+old[x,y+1]+old[x+1,y+1])/16
```

Enlarging by an Integer Factor

```
(x<X/5 && y<Y/5) ? old[x*5,y*5] : 0
```

Enlarges by a factor of 5

Shrinking by an Integer Factor

```
old[x/3,y/3]
```

Shrinks by a factor of 3

Mirroring

```
old[X-x,y]
```

Turning the Picture Upside Down

```
old[x,Y-y]
```

Rotating by 90° Clockwise

```
old[y,X-x]
```

Rotating by 90° Counterclockwise

```
old[Y-y,x]
```

Averaging Three Images

```
(one+two+three)/3
```

Weighted Average

```
(W1*one+W2*two+W3*three)/(W1+W2+W3)
```

Weight factors: W1, W2, W3

Relief

```
old-old[x+2,y+2]
```

Arbitrary Grid Transforms

See Chapter 4, photos 10, 11, and 13.

```
old[x+(64-(old%16)*(old%16))/8, y+(64-(old/16)*(old/16))/8]
old^(old*(128-(x-128)*(x-128)-(y-128)*(y-128)))>>17
old[x+(x%32)-16, y]
```

Transforms Using Trigonometric Functions

See Chapter 4, photo 12, and Chapter 3, expression 3.35.

```
old[x+sin(X*x/4)*X/8, y+sin(Y*y/4)*Y/8]
old[x+(X*cos(((x-X/2)*A)*2/X))/6, y]
```

Transforms Using Polar Coordinates

See Chapter 4, photos 1, 6, 8, 13, 14, and 19.

```
old[sqrt(r*R),~a]
old[r,~a+r/3]
old[x(a) * X/A, y(r) * Y/R]
old[x+((a+r/10)%32)-16, y]
old[(r*r)/R, a]
old[r,~a+old[r,a]/8]
```

Composites with Mattes

Straight composites of images, without averaging or fading, can be made in a number of different ways. In the examples below we use two images, named `I1` and `I2`, and the corresponding mattes, `M1` and `M2`. Assume that the images have the same background (e.g. portraits against a plain white background). At each point in the final image either `I1` or `I2` will be visible. All mattes are zero within the image area they define and `Z` outside of it. This type of image compositing is called the "Porter-Duff algebra."

```
(!M1)?I1:I2            I1 over I2
(!M2)?I2:I1            I2 over I1
(!M1&&!M2)?I1:0        I1 inside I2
(!M1&&!M2)?I2:0        I2 inside I1
(!M1&&!M2)?0:I1        I1 outside I2
(!M1&&!M2)?0:I2        I2 outside I1
(!M1&&!M2)?I1:I2       I1 atop I2
(!M1&&!M2)?I2:I1       I2 atop I1
```

The expressions are for non-blurred mattes (cf. Chapter 4 photo 3).

Arbitrary Composites

See Chapter 3, expressions 3.15, 3.28, 3.31, 3.32, and 3.33.

```
(one[x,y] > Z/2) ? one[x,y] : two[x,y]
(x>X/2)? old : old[X-x,y]
(x*two[x,y] + (X-x)*one[x,y])/X
(x<X/3)?two:(x>2*X/3)?one:((x-X/3)*one+(2*X/3-x)*two)*3/X
(y<Y/3)?two:(y>2*Y/3)?one:((y-Y/3)*one+(2*Y/3-y)*two)*3/Y
```

Plotting a Grid

```
(x%7>1)?(y%7>1)?0:Z:Z     Evenly spaced, thick white lines.
(x%7)?(y%7)?0:x/2:x/2     Thinner grid, fading from left to right.
```

Routine-1: Oil Transfer

An example library routine that can be linked with the image editor. This particular transformation was used for Chapter 4, photo 7. We will use the macro definitions for `New` and `Old` in also the other routines that are listed here.

```
#define N       3
#define New     src[CURNEW].pix
#define Old     src[CUROLD].pix

oil()
{       register int x, y;
        register int dx, dy, mfp;
        int histo[256];

        for (y = N; y < DEF_Y-N; y++)
        for (x = N; x < DEF_X-N; x++)
        {       for (dx = 0; dx < 256; dx++)
                        histo[dx] = 0;

                for (dy = y-N; dy <= y+N; dy++)
                for (dx = x-N; dx <= x+N; dx++)
                        histo[Old[dy][dx]]++;

                for (dx = dy = 0; dx < 256; dx++)
                        if (histo[dx] > dy)
                        {       dy = histo[dx];
                                mfp = dx;
                        }
                New[y][x] = mfp;
}       }
```

Note that the values in array histo can be updated faster if you avoid counting the same pixels more than once in a single sweep across the width of the image.

Routine-2: Picture Shear

See Chapter 4, photo 2. The routine uses a standard library function **rand()** to draw random numbers.

```
shear()
{       register int x, y, r;
        int dx, dy, yshift[DEF_X];

        for (x = r = 0; x < DEF_X; x++)
        {       if (rand()%256 < 128)
                        r--;
                else
                        r++;
                yshift[x] = r;
        }

        for (y = 0; y < DEF_Y; y++)
        {       if (rand()%256 < 128)
                        r--;
                else
                        r++;
```

```
                for (x = 0; x < DEF_X; x++)
                {       dx = x+r; dy = y+yshift[x];
                        if (dx >= DEF_X || dy >= DEF_Y
                        ||  dx < 0 || dy < 0)
                                continue;
                        New[y][x] = Old[dy][dx];
}       }       }
```

Routine-3: Slicing

See Chapter **4**, photo 9. For the definitions of `New` and `Old` see Routine-1.

```
slicer()
{       register int x, y, r;
        int dx, dy, xshift[DEF_Y], yshift[DEF_X];

        for (x = dx = 0; x < DEF_X; x++)
        {       if (dx == 0)
                {       r = (rand()&63)-32;
                        dx = 8+rand()&31;
                } else
                        dx--;
                yshift[x] = r;
        }
        for (y = dy = 0; y < DEF_Y; y++)
        {       if (dy == 0)
                {       r = (rand()&63)-32;
                        dy = 8+rand()&31;
                } else
                        dy--;
                xshift[y] = r;
        }

        for (y = 0; y < DEF_Y; y++)
        for (x = 0; x < DEF_X; x++)
        {       dx = x+xshift[y]; dy = y+yshift[x];
                if (dx < DEF_X && dy < DEF_Y
                &&  dx >= 0 && dy >= 0)
                        New[y][x] = Old[dy][dx];
}       }
```

Routine-4: Tiling

See also Chapter **4**, photo 15. The routine can be made more interesting by also randomly varying the size of the tiles.

```
#define T 25    /* tile size */

tiling()
{       register int x, y, dx, dy;
        int ox, oy, nx, ny;
```

```
        for (y = 0; y < DEF_Y-T; y += T)
        for (x = 0; x < DEF_X-T; x += T)
        {       ox = (rand()&31)-16;    /* displacement */
                oy = (rand()&31)-16;

                for (dy = y; dy < y+T; dy++)
                for (dx = x; dx < x+T; dx++)
                {       nx = dx+ox; ny = dy+oy;
                        if (nx >= DEF_X || ny >= DEF_Y
                        ||  nx < 0 || ny < 0)
                                continue;
                        New[ny][nx] = Old[dy][dx];
}       }       }
```

Routine-5: Melting

See Chapter 4, photo 5. This transformation "melts" the image in place. It does not use the edit buffer `new`, so the two buffers should not be swapped after the transformation completes.

```
melting()
{       register int x, y, val, k;

        for (k = 0; k < DEF_X*DEF_Y; k++)
        {       x = rand()%DEF_X;
                y = rand()%(DEF_Y-1);

                while (y < DEF_Y-1 && Old[y][x] <= Old[y+1][x])
                {       val = Old[y][x];
                        Old[y][x] = Old[y+1][x];
                        Old[y+1][x] = val;
                        y++;
}       }       }
```

Routine-6: Making a Matte

Image mattes were used, for instance, to make photos 2 and 19 in Chapter 4. For a portrait on a fairly light background, a first approximation of a matte can be made with the following routine. It will have to be touched up with a normal paint program. Experiment with different values for `G`.

```
#define G       7.5     /* gamma factor */

extern double pow();    /* the C-library routine */
matte()
{       register x, y;
        unsigned char lookup[256];

        for (x = 0; x < 256; x++)
                lookup[x] = (255. * pow(x/255., G)<3.)?255:0;
        for (y = 0; y < DEF_Y; y++)
        for (x = 0; x < DEF_X; x++)
                New[y][x] = lookup[Old[y][x]];
}
```

Photo Credits

The Cover

The cover image is a composite of two different portraits of New York artist Hillary Burnett. The original photographs were taken by the author with a 4×5 inch view camera on Polaroid film type 52. One of the photos was mirrored, combined with the original, and merged with the second. The entire composite can be expressed in the picture editing language introduced in this book and executed with the image editor discussed in Chapter 5.

Chapter 1

The *Mona Leo* picture on page 1 is a composite of the Mona Lisa and a mirror image of a self-portrait of Leonardo da Vinci, both scaled and lined up to make a perfect fit. Computer artist Lillian Schwartz (see Chapter 4, photo 19) and I made the composite using the picture editing language discussed in Chapter 2. More information on this image can be found in the special issue of the monthly *Arts & Antiques* of January 1987.

The foreground of the combination print on page 2 is an old transparent collodium glass positive by an unknown photographer. The background was computer generated, with a program written by Don Mitchell of AT&T Bell Labs, and matted in.

On page 4, the photo on the left is a collage made by John Heartfield in 1931. The full title of the work is *The Crisis Party Convention of the Social Democratic Party of Germany*. It can be found in, a.o., *John Heartfield Leben und Werk*, by Wieland Herzfelde, VEB Verlag der Kunst, Dresden, 3rd printing 1986, LSV-8116. The photo is reproduced here with permission from the Heartfield Archiv in Berlin and publisher VEB Verlag der Kunst in Dresden.

The photo on the right was made by Jerry Uelsmann in 1970. It is titled *The Little Hamburger Tree*. It appears, for instance, in his book *Silver Meditations*, Morgan & Morgan Publishing, Dobbs Ferry, N.Y., 1975, ISBN 0-871-00087-3. The photo is preproduced with permission of Jerry Uelsmann.

Chapter 2

The photo on the title page is a portrait of Doug McIlroy of AT&T Bell Labs, digitally faded from a negative to a positive. The original photo was made by Rob Pike.

Page 9. Willard S. Boyle and George E. Smith, demonstrating the first CCD television camera at Bell Labs in 1974. Photo courtesy of AT&T.

A photo of the Canon RC-701 still video image camera on page 10 is reproduced with permission from Canon U.S.A., Inc.

Chapter 3

The photo that opens this chapter is of Jim McKie, an employee of Bellcore, with a transformation similar to the one used for Chapter **4**, photo 6. Mckie's portrait was also used for the transformations on page 22 and 23. All photos in this chapter are from the series of 4×5 inch polaroids taken by Rob Pike (see the introduction to Chapter **4**). The only picture not taken by Rob is his own portrait, which was taken by the author.

Chapter 4

The first picture is the result a square root transformation (cf. photo 1 in this chapter) applied to the EWD icon, also shown on the same page.

Most photos in this chapter were taken by Rob Pike with a 4×5 inch view camera on Polaroid type 52 film. The exceptions are the following six photos.

The originals for photos 1 and 3 were made by Philippe Halsman, © Yvonne Halsman.

The original for photo 2 is a portrait of Alexander Graham Bell taken in 1876. The photograph is by Holton, courtesy and copyright of the Bell family and the National Geographic Society.

Photo 18, a portrait of Karen Nelson, is reprinted with permission from the *Bell Systems Technical Journal*, © 1969 by AT&T.
Photo 19 is a portrait of Lillian Schwartz taken by the author.
Photo 20 was taken in 1963. The photographer is not known.

Chapter 5

The photo at the top of page 75 is the result of a pixel smearing operation that uses an arbitrary other portrait from our database as an index. The operation is applied to a portrait of Don Mitchell, better known for his research in computer graphics and cryptography.

Chapter 6

The picture on page 109 is a transformed portrait of Peter Weinberger, but this time applied to only half of the image. Cf. photo 5 in Chapter **4**.

NAME INDEX